Paperback ISBN: 978-1-0369-1911-5

HardCover ISBN: 978-1-0369-1912-2

UNWINNABLE NO MORE

LEGAL DISCLAIMER

I did not set out to write a leadership book. My goal was to make sense of my journey—the wins, the failures, and the quiet moments of doubt that no one saw. These pages hold my reflections, the lessons I learned the hard way, and the truths I discovered when I was ready to quit. It is messy and imperfect, but so is the journey. If you are willing to walk it with me, I promise to be honest about every step along the way.

Real-life events inspired the content, but I have changed names, timelines, and details to protect privacy and confidentiality. If you recognise any similarities to actual people, companies, or organisations, it is purely coincidental.

I am sharing the strategies and perspectives in this book to help you learn and grow. They are based on my experiences and the lessons I have learned. However, I am not offering legal, financial, medical, or professional advice. I cannot be responsible for how you choose to interpret or use this information. Whatever decisions you make after reading this book are yours alone and if you need professional guidance, I encourage you to seek it from a qualified expert.

I learned that leadership is not just about strategy or vision. It is about integrity, about staying true to who you are even when it is difficult. Every choice I made came down to one question: Could I live with it? Could I lead in a way that respected my values, even if it meant taking the harder road? That is why every insight in this book comes from a place of honesty. For me, winning was never about outsmarting others—it was about leading with integrity and courage.

I have done my best to make sure the information in this book is accurate and relevant. But I know that business environments, corporate cultures, and personal circumstances can vary for everyone. What worked for me might not work the same way for you. I encourage you to carefully consider your own situation and seek expert advice if needed before applying any of the ideas I share.

By reading this book, you accept that I cannot be held responsible for any consequences, direct or indirect, arising from how you use the information in these pages. You are in control of how you apply these concepts and the choices you make are yours alone.

AMNA ZAIDI

UNWINNABLE NO MORE

PREFACE

It begins like this. A moment. Unassuming. Easily missed.

You are standing in a meeting, sitting at a desk, staring at a screen. The world around you hums with the ordinary—papers shuffled, emails sent, deadlines chased. And then it happens. A request. A challenge. A shift so subtle at first that you do not recognise its weight. But beneath the surface, something irreversible begins.

At first, you tell yourself you are simply responding to circumstances. Adjusting. Moving forward in the way people do. But the truth—the truth you only realise later—is that this is the moment when the rules of the game change. The moment when you stop playing by the guidelines written for you and start rewriting them entirely.

This is a book about those moments.

The ones that catch you off guard. The ones that demand more from you than you think you have to give. The ones where failure seems inevitable, where the ceiling feels too low, where every move feels like a step into uncertainty.

For most of my life, I believed in structure. In preparation. In the idea that the people who succeed are the ones who have the clearest plan. I was wrong.

Success—real success—is not about following a perfect path. It is about knowing what to do when there isn't one. It is about looking at a situation where the odds are stacked against you and deciding to play anyway. It is about realising that the ceiling you are staring at is not actually a ceiling, but rather a challenge disguised as a limit. If only you choose to see it that way.

This is not a book about traditional success. It is not a step-by-step guide, or a neatly packaged set of strategies designed to fit into a template. It is, instead, a conversation. A challenge. An invitation to rethink the way you see the game entirely.

Because the game? The one you think you are playing?

It was never built for you to win.

I learned this lesson the way most of us do—through trial, failure, and moments of gut-wrenching uncertainty. I have stood in rooms where I did not feel I belonged, been handed responsibilities I did not feel qualified for, and fought against limitations I did not realise I had been conditioned to accept.

I also learned that the people who create shifts and leave their mark are rarely the ones who wait to be ready.

They are the ones who move while still afraid. The ones who step into the unknown before certainty arrives. The ones who realise that the unwinnable game is not unwinnable at all—it just requires different rules.

This book is a blueprint for rewriting those rules.

It is built on real moments, real failures, and real decisions made in rooms where the stakes were too high, and the safety net had already disappeared. It is for anyone who has ever looked at the expectations placed upon them and thought: *Surely, there has to be another way.*

If you have ever felt like you were playing a game you could not win, this book is for you.

If you have ever been told to wait your turn, to prove yourself, to earn your seat before you speak, this book is for you.

If you have ever doubted your own ability but moved forward anyway, this book is for you.

You do not need permission to lead. You do not need guarantees to move.

You need only one thing:

A willingness to step forward.

The rest? You will build along the way.

Are you ready?

Dedication

In the name of Allah, the Most Gracious, the Most Merciful.

This book is a reflection of *tawakkul*—an Islamic concept rooted in the idea of trusting Him while doing everything in my power. With faith, surrender, and effort, I have learned that no challenge is impossible to overcome.

To my father, who left this world before I could write this book.

Losing you changed everything, but the lessons you left behind continue to light my path. Not a single day goes by without me thinking of you.

To my mother, the heart and soul of our family. You are the quiet force that has held us together, the example I turn to when I need to remember what true strength looks like. If I can be even a fraction of the woman you are, I will have done something right.

UNWINNABLE NO MORE

TABLE OF CONTENTS

Chapter 1: The Moment That Changed Everything --------- 16

Chapter 2: Challenge The Rules. Rewrite The Win --------- 38

Chapter 3: Growth In Discomfort ------------------------------ 78

Chapter 4: When The Game Is Rigged, Build Your Own 102

Chapter 5: The Breaking Point Before The Breakthrough 126

Chapter 6: The Ceiling That Wasn't A Ceiling ------------- 158

Chapter 7: What If I Fail? ------------------------------------- 188

Chapter 8: Leadership Unchained: Influence Without
Authority--- 212

Chapter 9: From Success To Significance: Crafting Your
Legacy--- 248

Chapter 10: When Giving Felt Like Losing ---------------- 270

Epilogue --- 292

Bibliography -- 300

About The Author -- 304

THE LESSONS THAT STAY WITH US

There are moments in life when time slows down, when the weight of a decision presses so heavily on your chest that it feels like the air has thinned, leaving you gasping for clarity. The world does not pause, but in that moment, everything sharpens—the voices in your head, the pounding in your chest, the raw, unfiltered uncertainty of not knowing whether stepping forward is the right move or whether holding back is the only thing keeping you from falling apart. These are the moments that define us. They force us to confront who we are and what we truly believe in. Moments that leave us breathless, shattered, questioning everything we thought we knew.

Moments that echo in the silence long after they've passed, reminding us of battles fought and wounds that never fully heal. I remember one of those moments vividly. I was standing in front of a room full of decision-makers, trying to speak with confidence while fighting the voice in my head that told me I didn't belong. My hands were shaking, my throat was tight, but I spoke anyway. When it was over, I walked out of that room feeling exposed, raw, like I had given too much of myself and still didn't know if it was enough.

Those moments leave scars. But they also build resilience. And it's in those scars that we find the strength to keep going. They demand answers when all we have are questions. They expose our deepest fears and reveal our truest selves. Moments that challenge us to rise above our fear or risk being consumed by it. We all have them and we all carry the wounds they leave behind. Ones that remind us of what we've survived, even when the world kept spinning as if nothing had changed. Because the world will always keep spinning. And these wounds—these scars—they tell the story of battles fought in silence, of resilience found in the depths of despair.

We have all been there. At the edge of something terrifying, uncertain, unfamiliar. Maybe it's standing at a crossroads, faced with a decision that could change everything. Or the crushing realisation that life, as you know it, would never be the same again. Or perhaps it is the quiet, invisible battles—the ones you fight alone, behind closed doors, when the weight of the world feels too heavy to bear. When the darkness feels suffocating and the silence becomes deafening. When you lie awake at night, staring at the ceiling, haunted by worries that refuse to rest. When the world outside seems oblivious to the storm raging within. We all carry burdens no one else can see. We wear smiles that hide struggles too complex to explain. We've mastered the art of pretending. Pretending to be okay when we're quietly falling apart. Pretending to be strong when we feel anything but. Pretending to move forward when we're stuck in the past.

Behind every smile is a story. Behind every silence is a struggle. And behind every tear is a truth we're too afraid to speak.

Maybe it was the moment you were forced to walk away from something you loved. Maybe it was when you had to fight for something no one else believed in. Maybe it was grief, loss, or the crushing weight of responsibility when you did not feel strong enough to carry it. These are the moments that strip us bare, the moments that force us to question everything—our choices, our strength, even our worth. They make us doubt our own voices, question our own value, and wonder whether we are enough. They leave us feeling exposed, raw, vulnerable. But they also reveal our hidden strength—the kind we never knew we had until we were forced to find it. These are the moments that make us feel small, insignificant. Moments that whisper lies of inadequacy, convincing us that we are not enough. But these are also the moments that forge us, shaping us into who we are meant to become.

I have lived those moments more times than I like to admit. Each time, when doubt and fear threatened to consume me, I turned to the lessons my father taught me.

Not written in books or spoken in grand speeches, but embedded in the way he lived, in the way he carried himself through storms without ever bending to them. He was my compass. The one I turned to for every piece of advice, for every uncertainty clouding my path. It did not matter how complex the problem was or how lost I felt; he was the constant I could always rely on.

In my professional journey, he was my silent partner, the unseen force behind every decision. When I questioned my strength, he reminded me of who I was. When I doubted my purpose, he showed me how to find it again. He showed me that courage is not the absence of fear, but the willingness to move forward despite it. That sometimes, strength is found not in the roar of confidence, but in the quiet resolve to keep going, even when the road is unclear. He never needed to raise his voice to teach me the most profound lessons. His wisdom was in his silence, his strength in his presence. He never needed to have all the answers. He just needed to be there. And somehow, that was enough. Enough to make me believe that I could face anything, as long as I wasn't facing it alone. But then, I had to learn how to be strong without him. Even now, when I feel the weight of the world pressing down, I still find myself searching for his voice, his calmness, his steadfast belief that I could withstand any storm.

Even in his most vulnerable days, he was unbreakable. When he faced his terminal diagnosis, he stood with a bravery that defied fear. He didn't know what the future held or how soon it would end, but he never let it defeat him. His courage was quiet, not boastful. He accepted his fate not because he was giving up, but because he understood the cycle of life. He was content with what life had blessed him with and he was ready to face the outcome that we, as his family, could not even comprehend. I often wondered how he found the strength to let go when I could barely hold on. I asked myself how he managed to find peace in his ending while I was still grappling with the thought of living without him. How he embraced the unknown with grace, while I was terrified of a future without his presence. It was only later that I realised: his courage wasn't in facing death, but in teaching us how to go on living.

He believed that real strength is forged in struggle—not in avoiding it, but in walking straight through it. That sacrifice is not something to be feared, but something to be understood, embraced, even respected. He taught me that doing the right thing would rarely be the easiest, most convenient, or most comfortable choice. But he also knew, with a conviction that never wavered, that it was the only choice worth making.

His lessons were never forced upon us. Even as his days grew numbered, his presence remained unwavering. He exemplified strength not by fighting the inevitable, but by accepting it with grace. He did not like to see us cry and I often found myself hiding my tears behind his arm, not wanting him to see the pain I couldn't bear. I knew he was hurting too, but he was preparing us as best as he could for the life that would continue after he was gone.

In his last days, he gave us his final teachings—simple but profound: "Look after each other and pray for me," he said. That was it. A perspective so powerful that it made the unbearable seem almost manageable. He did not need to say much, because his life already spoke for him. His legacy is not just in the lessons he taught me, but in the way he lived them. It's in his quiet strength, his unwavering faith, his selfless love. It's in the way he faced the end, knowing that his story would continue through us. It's in every choice I make, every battle I fight, every victory I claim—because his courage lives on in me. His belief in strength was not about force, not about dominance—it was about resilience. He would remind me, in a voice that never lost its calm, that true strength is not in the body. It is in the mind. It is the ability to see clearly when everything is uncertain. It is the discipline to hold back when needed and the courage to step forward when it matters most.

7

When he was alive, he was the one person I turned to when my world felt unsteady. He had a way of making things simpler, of cutting through the noise and showing me that most impossible decisions were only impossible because of fear.

And then, one day, he was gone. Just like that.

Those days—the days that can never be erased from my memory—remain vivid and haunting. I watched him face the end with a courage that defied fear, a bravery that left me speechless. He was ready to embark on a journey to the hereafter with confidence and faith, even as it shattered us to watch him go. In his final days, he taught me how to face the unknown, how to navigate the darkest moments with dignity. His strength was not in resisting life's end but in embracing its purpose.

Even now, his voice echoes through my decisions, his courage sustaining me when I feel like falling apart. He saw solutions where I saw obstacles. And when I finally made it through the challenges I thought I could never overcome, he was never surprised. He had seen my strength long before I had. His pride was never loud, never boastful—but it was unshakable, and I held onto it like a lifeline.

Losing him felt like losing gravity. Like my entire world was nothing but a rug that'd been pulled from beneath my feet. The world that once had order became unpredictable. The ground beneath me, once steady, cracked open and I found myself falling through the spaces he had once held together. In my darkest moments, I was surrounded by people but had never felt more alone. He was the one who had always known what to do and now, for the first time, I had to find my way without him.

Grief is a language we all understand, even if our losses are different. Whether it's the death of a loved one, the end of a relationship, or the loss of a dream, the pain is universal. It shatters your sense of normalcy, leaving you to piece together a new reality. If you have ever lost something you could never replace, then you already know my pain. And I already know yours. Because grief is the price we pay for love. And the deeper the love, the greater the pain. Yet, in that pain, we find the echoes of what was once beautiful. In that void, we carry forward the legacy of those we've lost.

Even in his absence, he was with me. His words lingered in the quiet spaces of my mind, becoming my anchor when everything else felt uncertain." My father's final words, spoken before he left this world, remain etched into my soul:

"Consistency and the pursuit of the greater objective in life—that is the true meaning of success. Doing the right

thing will not always be easy, but if you are standing for the truth, there is nothing to fear."

I clung to those words, repeating them when the weight of loss threatened to pull me under. Losing him was one of the greatest challenges of my life—a moment that felt utterly unwinnable. But through that pain, I discovered a strength I did not know I had.

Grief, like any great challenge, strips away pretence. It forces us to confront who we are and what truly matters. And it was in those moments of overwhelming loss—when I had nothing left to hold onto—that I found new meaning in *tawakkul*.

Tawakkul is not just trust. It is the ultimate surrender. The balance between doing everything in your power and releasing control over what is beyond you. It is knowing that while you are responsible for your effort, the outcome has never been—and never will be—in your hands. It is understanding that no struggle, no hardship, no moment of pain is meaningless. It is the belief that every tear is seen, every prayer is heard, and every trial has a purpose. That even when life seems to be falling apart, there is a greater plan unfolding, one that we may not yet understand. That even in our worst moments, we are never truly alone.

This realisation became my lifeline. It was what I turned to when I felt like I could not go on.

And it is what I want to share with you in this book.

Because this book is not just about loss. It is not just about struggle, or perseverance, or faith. It is about what happens when we decide to rise above our fear, when we embrace the challenges that were meant to break us and use them to build something greater. It is about what is possible when we trust—not in ourselves alone, but in something far beyond us.

I know you carry burdens no one else sees. I know there are days when you question whether you have the strength to go on. I know because I have walked through that darkness, too. This book is not here to diminish your pain, but to stand with you in it. Because I know what it's like to carry burdens that feel too heavy to bear. I know the exhaustion of fighting battles no one else can see. I know the loneliness of suffering in silence, pretending to be okay when the weight of the world is crushing you. I know the pain of longing for someone who can't come back. And I know the courage it takes to keep going, even when you feel like giving up.

This book is also about *you*. Because I know you're carrying pain that words can't fully describe. I know there are nights when you feel like breaking, when the silence is too loud and the darkness too suffocating. I know there are mornings when getting out of bed feels like the hardest thing you will ever do. But I want you to know this. Your pain is real, but so is your strength.

This book is an invitation to look at your own unwinnable moments. To reflect on the times when life tested you, when you questioned your strength, your purpose, your ability to keep going. To recognise that those moments did not define you but shaped you. That what felt like breaking was actually the beginning of rebuilding something stronger.

If you are holding this book in your hands, it is because some part of you is searching for something. Maybe you want clarity. Maybe you want strength. Maybe you just want to know that you are not alone. Whatever it is, I want you to know this: You are capable of more than you have ever imagined.

Your struggles are not punishments. They are training. They are shaping you into the person you are meant to become. And no matter how impossible things feel at this moment, no matter how heavy the weight of your burden, you are not alone in carrying it.

With every word in these pages, I hope you see what I have seen. That loss does not mean the end. That fear is not a stop sign. That every challenge, every hardship, every moment of uncertainty is an opportunity to become something greater than you ever thought possible.

And most importantly, that *with Allah, nothing is impossible.*

This is not just my story—it's ours. It's about every unwinnable moment that tried to break us. It's about every time we chose to rise instead of fall. And if you're still standing, even when the world tried to bury you, then this story belongs to you, too. And it is just beginning.

Because this is a story of rising. Of finding light in the darkness and strength in surrender. It's about rewriting the rules and redefining what it means to win, even when the odds are stacked against you.

And as you turn these pages, my hope is that you find your way through the unwinnable too. Because this is not about surviving the storm—it's about learning to dance in the rain. It's about finding beauty in the brokenness, strength in the struggle, hope in the hurt. It's about rising after every fall, healing after every heartbreak, and rebuilding after every loss. And if you're still fighting, even when the world tries to break you, then your story is not over. It's just beginning.

Because if you're still here, if you're still fighting, then you've already survived the worst. And that makes you stronger than you realise. This story is a testament to resilience. To finding hope when all seems lost. And to the undeniable truth that no matter how broken you feel, you are never beyond healing.

Life is a movie—a series of moments stitched together to tell a story. Some scenes make us laugh while others make us cry. Some leave us breathless, while others teach us how to breathe again.

Every moment matters. Every scene has a purpose. So, take a seat. Get comfortable. Turn the page. And let the movie begin. I hope you enjoy it.

CHAPTER 1

THE MOMENT THAT CHANGED EVERYTHING

———•○◇○•———

I t was a gloomy Friday afternoon in London, the kind where the sky is an indistinct shade of steel, pressing down on the city like an afterthought. The air carried a stillness that signalled the end of the week—emails sent, calendars checked, coffee cups half-finished and forgotten on desks. I was sitting at mine, methodically ticking off the last few tasks on my list, grateful for the predictability of routine. There was something satisfying about the finality of small completions: an inbox cleared, a report submitted, a quiet exhale of knowing that—at least for now—there were no fires left to put out.

Then the news broke.

It came as a whisper at first, an overheard fragment of conversation that made the air in the office change. A sudden shift in leadership. An executive removed—no explanation, no warning, just the rapid unravelling of stability in a place that had, moments before, felt immovable. Hushed voices spread the uncertainty across the floor like a slow-moving current. Some claimed it had been planned. Others swore it had been abrupt. Either way, the effect was the same. You could feel the energy tightening around you, an invisible force pressing against your skin.

I tried to focus on my work, but it was like trying to hold onto water. The familiar routine, the one I had counted on just moments ago, now felt like a thin illusion stretched over something much deeper. My hands hovered over the keyboard, but my mind was already in free-fall, tracing the possibilities of what had happened behind closed doors. Leadership changes didn't just happen overnight—not like this. This had been in motion long before today, which meant the company had known before we did. And if they could keep something that big under wraps, what else were they keeping?

Then came the call.

"Amna, the CFO wants to see you. Now."

The words, though simple, landed like a stone in my stomach. The CFO? That wasn't routine. No one was summoned to the CFO's office casually and certainly not at the end of a Friday. There was something unsettling about it—the precision, the urgency, the absence of explanation. My mind went straight to the worst-case scenario. *Was I about to be let go? Was my role affected by this shake-up?*

I stood, smoothing the front of my blazer in a gesture that felt like an act of control, but my hands betrayed me with a slight tremor. Around me, the office continued in its usual rhythm—people at their desks, fingers clacking against keyboards, conversations murmuring in the background. Yet I felt untethered, as if I were moving through the space as an outsider, a foreigner in my own environment.

The walk to the lift felt longer than it should have. I became hyperaware of the details I had ignored all day— the artificial glow of the overhead lights, the faint smell of burnt coffee lingering from the break room, the way the carpeted floor muted my footsteps. My mind oscillated between forced rationality and creeping dread. Maybe this was just a briefing. Maybe I was overthinking. But the other possibility—that this conversation would upend my career—refused to loosen its grip.

There's a peculiar thing that happens when you step into a lift alone in a moment of uncertainty—everything else seems to shrink.

The mirrored walls reflected an image of me that I wasn't sure I recognised—poised on the outside, but unravelling beneath the surface. My fingers clenched around my notebook, knuckles whitening against the leather cover. A small detail, but a telling one. I was holding on to something solid, something tangible, as if that could anchor me. My reflection stared back, eyes slightly widened, a flicker of unease betraying the carefully composed expression I had trained myself to wear.

The logical part of my brain attempted to run defence. *Maybe it's nothing. Maybe they need your input on something routine. Maybe this is an opportunity, not a threat.* But logic is a weak opponent against fear. Because fear isn't interested in probabilities—it is only interested in survival. And survival means preparing for the worst.

What if I was about to be blindsided? What if this was one of those moments where a single decision made behind closed doors rewrote the trajectory of your career? My breath came slower, measured, as I forced myself to stay composed.

The lift hummed as it ascended. It wasn't just the movement that made my stomach turn; it was the sense that, in the span of seconds, I was about to cross an invisible threshold into something irreversible. By the time the doors opened with a soft chime, I had braced myself for impact.

Stepping onto the executive floor felt like stepping into a different reality.

Everything was muted here. The usual sounds of the office—the ringing phones, the steady hum of conversation—were absent. The air itself felt heavier, thicker with something intangible. Authority had a way of altering even the acoustics of a space.

The carpet softened the impact of my heels, making my movements unnervingly silent. I approached the assistant's desk. She glanced up from her stack of papers, offering a polite smile paired with an unreadable nod before gesturing toward the closed door of the CFO's office. No unnecessary pleasantries. No indication of what awaited me inside. It was as if I were walking in there completely blindfolded.

My stomach coiled tighter as I took the final steps toward the door and shut it behind me. I was inside.

The room was expansive, framed by floor-to-ceiling windows that stretched across one side, revealing a panoramic view of London's skyline. The city spread out beyond the glass, its movement ceaseless, unconcerned with the small dramas unfolding within these walls. But I wasn't looking at the view.

I was looking at him.

The CFO sat behind a sleek, imposing desk, his presence measured and controlled. His expression was unreadable—neither warm nor unwelcoming, just deliberate. That, more than anything, put me on edge.

"Amna, take a seat," he said, gesturing to the chair across from him.

I lowered myself into it, gripping the armrests as though they might steady me. My heart pounded, but I willed myself to maintain eye contact, to appear unaffected.

Then came the words that would alter everything.

"We need someone to take over the programme," he said. "It's high-profile, high-stakes, and vital to the company. I'd like you to lead it."

For a second, my mind refused to process it.

I had walked into this room bracing for bad news. Maybe even preparing to justify my position in the company. But I had not prepared for this. And now, I was being asked to be that leadership. I swallowed, my mind racing between two questions.

Why me?

Can I actually do this?

The CFO had finished speaking, but the silence between us had only just begun.

I gripped the armrests of my chair, trying to assemble a coherent response, but my mind felt like a machine jamming under the weight of an impossible input.

I was being offered a role that would not only define my career, but also put me in uncharted waters. A high-profile, multi-million-pound programme with government scrutiny, razor-thin margins for error, and real-world consequences. And somehow, at 24, I was the one they had chosen.

There had to be someone else—someone older, more experienced, someone who looked the part.

Stepping into leadership meant more than taking on responsibility. It meant redefining the very image of what a leader looked like. It meant embracing a role where I didn't fit the mould—not just because of my age or experience, but because of everything else that made me who I was. I felt the weight of representation, the pressure to excel so that the door would stay open for others who looked like me. And yet, I knew that if I hesitated, if I let the fear of being different dictate my choices, I would prove every doubter right. Aside from propelling my career forward, this was about paving a path that didn't exist before.

My breath was steady, but inside, doubt coiled tightly, winding itself around every thought.

I glanced up at the CFO, searching for something—a hesitation, a trace of uncertainty that might indicate that this was some kind of test rather than a decision already made. But there was nothing. His face remained unreadable, his posture composed.

He had already decided.

I was the only one questioning it.

Doubt doesn't arrive loudly. It doesn't storm into the room announcing itself. Instead, it seeps in through the smallest cracks, whispering just loud enough to distort reality.

I could feel it now, slithering its way through my thoughts.

They've made a mistake.

They think you're something you're not.

You're just lucky to be here.

Imposter syndrome at its finest.

I had battled these voices before, but they had never been as loud as they were now. And they weren't just internal. They were echoes of real things I had seen and felt.

I wasn't white.

I wasn't middle-aged.

I wasn't male.

And I wasn't the person most people pictured when they thought of a high-stakes leader.

I had spent my career watching how power naturally flowed toward those who fit the mould. I had seen opportunities handed to people who didn't have to prove their competence before they were trusted with it. I had seen how easily experience was assumed for some, while others had to demonstrate it over and over.

And yet, here I was.

There are moments in life when you are forced to confront a fundamental truth about yourself. Not the polished version, not the one you present to the world, but the raw, unfiltered version that dictates what you really believe. I had worked too hard, too deliberately, to just accept a seat at the table without questioning the terms.

The CFO leaned forward slightly, his elbows resting on the desk, his fingers laced together in a way that signalled deliberation.

"This programme has been under immense scrutiny," he said. "There's no room for error."

I nodded, but the weight of what he was saying pressed down hard.

Multi-million-pound project.

Affecting multiple markets.

Regulator oversight.

And then the part that sent a chill through my spine.

"The penalty for non-compliance is a three-year prison sentence for the accountable executives."

The words landed slowly, deliberately, as if they had to be absorbed piece by piece. Three years. My eyes flickered to the polished wood of his desk, as if somewhere in the grains of the surface, I could find a way out of this moment. This wasn't just about reputation or career trajectory. This was about stepping into a role where failure wasn't just a professional setback—it was catastrophic.

I thought about what this would mean. What most people don't realise is that in financial services, certain programmes carry personal liability. Under regulatory regimes like the Senior Managers and Certification Regime (SMCR), executives can be held criminally accountable if a programme under their oversight fails to meet legal or regulatory standards. It's not about being involved in wrongdoing. It's about being responsible—

by name and by role. And this was the role I was stepping into.

The CFO continued, his voice measured. "You'll have executive oversight, but this is your responsibility."

There it was again. *Your responsibility.* The weight of those two words settled like stone in my chest. There was no undoing this moment. No pretending I hadn't heard him. No turning back to the version of myself who had walked into this room only expecting a routine meeting. I exhaled slowly, keeping my expression neutral. Because there was no avoiding it now.

Whether I wanted it or not, this was mine to carry.

The silence between us stretched, heavy and full of unspoken meaning. This was the kind of opportunity that either catapults you into a different orbit or consumes you entirely. There is no middle ground. Take it and you enter a league that only a few ever get to see. Hesitate and someone else will take the seat you weren't ready for. The battle between hesitation and action raged inside me.

And then, a different voice spoke.

It wasn't the voice of fear. It wasn't the voice of doubt. It was a question, calm and clear.

What if you are ready?

26

Not a declaration. Not a reassurance. Just a question. And somehow, that was enough. I straightened slightly, adjusting my posture, grounding myself in the weight of my own decision.

Leadership doesn't wait for you to feel ready. It demands you step into responsibility before you believe you're capable of carrying it. I had always assumed that confidence came first—that leaders acted because they were sure of themselves. But that was the myth. Real leadership meant moving forward while still questioning your place. It meant showing up even when the doubt was deafening. I wasn't just learning how to lead—I was learning how to belong. This meant trusting that the One who called you to this moment would carry you through it. And I was learning what it meant to surrender, not in defeat, but in trust. This was *tawakkul* in action.

"I'll do it," I said. My voice did not waver.

But then, before the moment could slip away, I added one more thing.

"And I'd like the same salary as my predecessor."

The words had already left my mouth. There was no taking them back. The CFO's expression did not change. And that silence—those few extra seconds of nothing—were the longest of my life. The urge to backtrack rose instinctively.

27

You shouldn't have said that.

You've overstepped.

You've ruined it.

I could feel my pulse hammering against my ribs. My hands remained still, but I was gripping the chair slightly tighter than before. This was the moment where people usually folded. Where they softened the request. Where they laughed nervously and said, *I mean, if that's possible, of course.* Where they tried to take the words back before they had the chance to be rejected.

I didn't move. I let the words sit there. And then, finally, he spoke.

"Okay," he said simply. "We'll do that."

The relief should have been immediate. But instead, something else settled in. A realisation. The world doesn't give you what you deserve. It gives you what you have the courage to ask for. And what you have the resilience to back up with action. That moment was about proving to myself that the rules had never been real. Because in those few seconds, the version of myself that had walked into this room no longer existed.

The CFO had agreed—no hesitation, no negotiation, no justification required. I had spoken and it had been accepted. And yet, instead of relief, something heavier settled in. Because now, there was no turning back. The moment I walked out of this office, I would no longer be just another employee working in the shadows. I would be the leader of a multi-million-pound programme, a position carrying immense scrutiny and risk. It was the kind of responsibility that forced you to walk differently, to speak differently, to see yourself in a way that no longer fit the person you were moments ago.

I stood, pushing my chair back with slow, deliberate movements. It felt necessary to move with precision now, to maintain the illusion that I had already accepted this new version of myself.

I often wondered what he saw in me. For some reason, he chose to believe in what could be, not just what was. And in doing so, he taught me that real leadership is about vision, not validation.

The CFO extended his hand and as I shook it, I could feel the firmness of his grip, the silent weight of expectation. "Good. We'll set up a formal briefing first thing Monday," he said.

I nodded, swallowing the instinct to hesitate. "I'll be ready." A lie. Because in that moment, I wasn't sure I had ever felt less ready for anything in my life.

Stepping out of his office, I expected the air to feel different, for the world outside to have shifted in response to what had just happened inside that room. But it hadn't. The executive floor remained exactly as it had been before—quiet, controlled, utterly indifferent to the transformation that had just occurred. The assistant who had nodded me in glanced up as I walked past, her expression neutral, professional. For a fleeting second, I wondered whether she knew. Whether she had been aware of what that meeting had been about. Whether she had seen enough of these moments unfold to recognise the subtle shift in someone who had just stepped into a new version of themselves. Probably not. But *I* knew. And that was enough.

I stepped into the lift and pressed the button for my floor, watching as the doors slid shut, enclosing me in the same mirrored walls that had reflected my anxiety on the way up. But now, something had changed. I didn't look away this time. I held my own gaze, studying the face staring back at me. I had walked into that meeting as one version of myself and walked out as another. But the shift was not complete yet.

Moments like this don't feel the way you expect them to. You think that when you finally break through a barrier, when you claim something that once felt unattainable, the world will acknowledge it. You think there will be some external signal, a dramatic shift in the air, a sign that marks the before and after. But the truth is, these moments arrive in silence. There is no music swelling in the background, no validation offered by the universe. Just a quiet realisation that the person you were five minutes ago no longer exists and the only person who will ever truly understand the gravity of that shift is you.

As the lift descended, I let the silence teach me something. That power is not something given. It is something taken. That the real test wasn't in whether I had *been* chosen for this role—it was in whether I would *own* it.

By the time I reached my desk, the office had already moved on. I sat down, placing my notebook beside my keyboard, staring at the screen in front of me as if I could will myself back into the rhythm of before.

But before was now of another realm.

I reached for my pen, intending to jot down a few thoughts, but my hand hesitated over the blank page. What was there to say? How do you write about a moment that has altered everything, when you don't yet know how to speak the language of the person you are becoming? I exhaled slowly and instead wrote two words at the top of the page:

Monday morning.

The first step.

Here's what nobody tells you about stepping into a new reality: the fear doesn't disappear. People assume that once you "arrive"—once you get the title, the salary, the authority—confidence follows automatically. It doesn't. If anything, the fear gets louder. The difference is that it no longer whispers doubts about whether you can do something—it starts whispering about *whether you can sustain it.*

I could have spent the weekend spiralling, questioning every single aspect of this decision. And trust me, I was tempted to. The easy thing would have been to sit in that uncertainty, to let the fear convince me that I had somehow gotten away with something, that on Monday, they would see through me and realise their mistake. But then, a thought stopped me.

What if I just focused on the next step?

Not the entire programme. Not the pressure of leading a team. Not the potential failure that could unravel everything. Just. The. Next. Step.

Fear thrives on the enormity of the unknown. It magnifies the distance between where you are and where you need to be, making it seem impossible to bridge the gap.

32

But *you never have to jump the entire distance at once.* You only ever have to take one step. And then another. And then another.

I grabbed a blank sheet of paper and wrote:

MONDAY MORNING: FIRST MOVES.

Underneath, I listed three things:

1. Meet with the project team.
2. Understand key risks.
3. Identify what I need to learn first.

That was it. No grand plan, no overcomplication. Just a path forward. Because confidence isn't something you wait for. It's something you create.

The moment I wrote those words, the fear loosened its grip just slightly. Not enough to disappear, but enough for me to recognise that it didn't have to dictate what I did next. That weekend, I learned something that would shape the rest of my career: You don't become competent before taking action. You take action and that's what makes you competent.

Nobody feels ready.

Not the CEO stepping into their first major acquisition.

Not the writer staring at a blank manuscript.

Not the athlete before the final race.

Readiness? It's a myth.

The real game is about momentum. You start. You make mistakes. You learn. You adapt. And somewhere in that process, *you become the person who can handle it.*

It wasn't the act of being placed in this position that made me a leader. It wasn't the title, the salary, or the authority. It was the moment I *chose to lead.* That moment didn't happen in the CFO's office, or when I negotiated my salary, or even when I stepped into the room that morning. It happened when I decided that I wouldn't shrink under the weight of expectation. That I wouldn't waste energy convincing myself that I was unqualified. That I wouldn't wait for external validation to believe that I belonged.

We like to think that leadership comes from experience, from credentials, from time spent accumulating knowledge until we are finally ready. But leadership happens in an instant. It happens the moment you stop waiting for someone to give you permission. The moment you step into responsibility before you feel ready. Because readiness is not a requirement for action—action is what creates readiness.

That meeting was the first of many—the first of countless decisions, conflicts, and moments where I would be tested. And yet, I knew that this moment—the first one—was the most important. Not because it was the hardest, but because it was the one that determined how I would face everything that followed.

Looking back, it's easy to see that meeting with the CFO as a turning point. But honestly, that moment wasn't what changed me. What changed me was what I did with it. Because everyone has moments that could alter the course of their lives. The real question is not whether those moments will come; it's whether we will have the courage to step into them when they do.

This is the lesson I wish someone had told me earlier: *You don't have to feel ready to act. You act first and then you become ready.* Every person who has ever achieved something meaningful has done so while battling the same fear, the same doubts, the same voice that whispers, "You are not enough." The difference is that they move anyway.

And so do you.

Take a moment to think about your own life. What decisions, what opportunities, what responsibilities have you hesitated to claim because you believed you needed more experience, more knowledge, more certainty? Write it down. Acknowledge it. And then, make a choice. Because waiting doesn't eliminate fear; it only delays the life you were meant to step into.

Now, commit to one bold move. One action that you will take this week, despite the uncertainty. Don't wait until the fear is gone. Move while it's still there.

Because the unwinnable? It's not the end.

It's the beginning.

CHAPTER 2

CHALLENGE THE RULES.

REWRITE THE WIN.

———•◇•———

T he weight of the CFO's words didn't hit me all at once. It arrived in waves.

I spent most of Saturday waiting for a moment that never came—a sudden breakthrough, a shift where I would *feel* like the person capable of taking this on. Instead, I found myself reading through old project documents, analysing meeting transcripts and mentally running through every possible outcome. None of it gave me the certainty I was looking for.

By Sunday morning, something else settled in—a kind of quiet realisation. Maybe leadership wasn't about certainty. Maybe it was about moving forward despite the unknowns.

I sat at my kitchen table, coffee growing cold, staring at the company's project roadmap spread out in front of me. The lines of deadlines, dependencies, and milestones all neatly laid out—except, none of them mattered anymore. Half of them had already been missed. The other half were optimistic guesses at best. The entire thing felt less like a structured plan and more like a list of promises that had been broken before they even had a chance to be met.

Then it became clear: This wasn't just any project. We were in the middle of a financial controls remediation programme—an initiative born out of new legislation. In simple terms, the government had passed rules to tighten up financial practices, ensuring that companies like ours operated with robust safeguards against errors, fraud, or mismanagement. In its first year of compliance, every process was under the microscope, and our old ways of doing things simply wouldn't cut it anymore.

The realisation was sharp: *This is why the programme is failing. We're holding onto a plan that was never built for reality.*

I ran my fingers along the edges of the document, tracing the lines of an outdated strategy. The answer had been in front of me the whole time. The only way forward wasn't through salvaging this. It was through replacing it.

I exhaled, setting the papers aside. A new kind of clarity settled in—not the kind that came from having all the answers, but the kind that came from finally letting go of the wrong ones.

Monday morning arrived and with it, an unspoken decision: If I was going to do this, I had to step into it fully. Not cautiously. Not with one foot still in the door, waiting to retreat. But entirely.

I moved through the space with purpose, knowing the responsibility was now mine. But as I walked through the office hallways, I noticed something—the way I carried myself, the way I greeted people, the way I moved through the space. It wasn't forced and it wasn't performative. It was just a quiet understanding that, whether I liked it or not, I was the one people would be looking to now.

Leadership wasn't something I was waiting to be handed anymore. It was something I had already stepped into.

And that shift? It changed everything.

The tension was there the moment I entered the conference room.

Not the kind of tension that comes from confrontation, from people ready to challenge or resist. This was something quieter, heavier. The exhaustion of a team that had been fighting a losing battle for too long. The kind of silence that settles when people no longer expect things to change.

I took my seat at the head of the table. A simple action. Barely noticeable. And yet, it mattered.

Leadership is claimed through action, not granted through title. You don't linger at the door. You don't hesitate. You own the space.

Still, there was a flicker of hesitation inside me. A small voice whispering, *What if you're wrong? What if they're right—what if this is unsalvageable?*

I met the eyes of the people around the table. Senior stakeholders. Compliance officers. Regional leads. Some had already checked out, distancing themselves from the wreckage. Others watched with cautious scepticism, waiting to see if I was just another person walking into the fire.

I reached for the printed project roadmap.

A document revised so many times that it barely resembled the original. A plan adjusted, rewritten, patched up after every failure, every missed milestone, every attempt to course-correct without truly addressing the problem.

I hesitated for a fraction of a second.

A pause. A breath.

Then, I picked it up—and tore it in half.

The sound sliced through the silence like a clean blade.

A flicker of movement at the far end of the table. A compliance officer straightened in his chair. A regional lead blinked.

I set the torn halves of the roadmap on the table in front of me. Not aggressively. Not theatrically. Just deliberately.

Then I leaned forward slightly, my voice calm but unwavering.

"Let's stop pretending this is working."

Silence.

But now, it was different.

This wasn't the silence of people who had already checked out. This wasn't the silence of exhaustion anymore.

This was the silence of people waiting to hear what came next.

I let the moment stretch for a second longer before I spoke again.

"This project isn't failing because people aren't working hard enough. It's failing because we're measuring success in ways that don't apply anymore."

I saw the shift happen—small, almost imperceptible. A regional manager uncrossing her arms. A senior compliance officer leaning forward slightly.

It wasn't full buy-in. Not yet. But it was interest. And interest?

Interest was the first step toward belief.

Here's the thing about failing systems: they don't collapse because people stop trying. They collapse because the rules they are built on no longer match reality. That was the real issue here.

The original project plan had been built on a fantasy. A rigid timeline that assumed no obstacles, no unexpected delays, no complexity beyond what had been neatly mapped out in boardrooms. The success metrics were outdated compliance checkpoints—designed to ensure that we stayed within pre-existing frameworks, even when those frameworks had already failed us. The accountability structure wasn't about adaptation. It was about blame. Teams weren't experimenting or adjusting because they couldn't afford to. The cost of failure was too high. No one was taking risks. They were just covering themselves.

43

This wasn't a game we were losing. This was a game that had been rigged against us from the beginning. And my job wasn't to play it better.

It was to rewrite the game entirely.

There is a peculiar silence that follows an irreversible act. Not the absence of noise, but the kind of quiet that carries weight. The kind that means something has shifted.

I continued, "The plan we were following was never designed to survive this level of complexity," I continued. "The systems we're using weren't built for this scale. The reason you're exhausted—the reason this has felt impossible—is because it was impossible."

I paused again, scanning the room.

"And now that we've acknowledged that, we can actually do something about it."

Denial is the biggest obstacle to change. You can't solve a problem while still pretending it doesn't exist. And until this moment, that's exactly what had been happening. People were rearranging the furniture inside a burning house, hoping that if they adjusted things just right, the flames would put themselves out. They wouldn't.

The most dangerous thing about a failing system is that it convinces you it's still worth saving. It gives you just enough small wins to keep you trapped. Just enough progress to keep you invested. And in the process, it blinds you to the truth—that the system itself is the problem.

I leaned forward slightly, my voice unwavering.

"We need to stop pretending we're in control of everything. That's not what gets results. What matters is being able to move, even when things aren't clear."

That was the shift we needed to make. Not rigid planning. Not flawless execution. But agility. Adaptation. The ability to rethink the rules in real-time.

One of the senior leads cleared his throat. I could tell he was about to challenge me—not aggressively, not confrontationally, but in the way people do when they're trying to make sense of something that feels uncomfortable.

"Okay," he said, his voice carefully neutral. "But what exactly are you proposing? Because ripping up a plan is easy. Replacing it is harder."

I nodded. It was a fair challenge.

"This isn't about replacing it," I said. "This is about replacing how we think about success."

I stood, moving toward the whiteboard behind me. Picking up a marker, I wrote three words in bold, deliberate strokes:

Innovation

Adaptability

Momentum

I turned back to them.

"These are our new metrics."

There was a slight pause before someone exhaled, a short, sceptical breath.

I raised my hand before they could object.

"I know what you're thinking. This sounds like theory. It sounds nice—but it doesn't actually solve our execution problem." I tapped the marker against the board, once, twice. "But that's exactly the issue. We've been prioritising the wrong things. We've been measuring success by how well we adhere to a broken system, instead of whether we're actually moving forward."

I pointed to the first word.

Innovation.

"This means we stop trying to make the old system work. We test, we experiment, we create something new. We stop following rules just because they've existed for a long time."

I moved to the second.

Adaptability.

"This means we stop treating setbacks as failures. We stop acting like an unexpected problem is the end of the world. We course-correct fast and we keep moving."

And then, the third.

Momentum.

"This is the most important one. We don't wait for perfection before we act. We don't spend six months writing reports about why something isn't working. We make decisions quickly, even if they're messy, because the real danger isn't failure."

I underlined the word twice.

"The real danger is standing still."

Interest was building. I could feel it in the atmosphere. In the subtle body language of all those who sat before me. And this interest would soon morph into belief.

"Now," I said, lowering the marker, "if we're going to move, we need to decide what we're letting go of."

I gestured to the shredded roadmap on the table.

"Because here's the hard truth: Some of the things we've been holding onto? They're dead weight. And if we don't drop them now, they'll sink us later."

Silence.

Then, slowly, one of the senior managers spoke up.

"The regional rollout deadlines," she said. "They were set months ago. We keep pushing to meet them, but they don't match reality anymore."

I nodded.

"Then let's kill them," I said. "What else?"

Another voice.

"The compliance reporting process. We're so focused on tracking meaningless progress that it's slowing down actual execution."

"Gone," I said.

Someone else.

"The weekly status reports. They take hours to prepare and no one actually reads them."

"Dead," I said.

And just like that, the floodgates opened.

One by one, the outdated, ineffective systems started falling away. And with each one, you could feel it—the collective exhale of a team that had been suffocating under their own processes.

This wasn't just about cutting inefficiencies. This was about giving them permission to stop following broken rules.

And that?

That was freedom.

The Resistance and How to Overcome It

At first, change feels like a current pulling everything forward—fast, undeniable, unstoppable. People get caught in the energy of it, swept up in the thrill of a new way of doing things. But then, just when it feels like the shift is inevitable, the real battle begins. Because systems do not break quietly.

By Monday morning the following week, the pushback arrived.

The first sign was the emails—thinly veiled inquiries from senior executives, their language as precise as a scalpel, carefully probing for weak points.

"Why were deadlines removed?"

"How will you ensure accountability without weekly reports?"

"Who signed off on these decisions?"

I let them sit in my inbox for a moment, reading between the lines. These weren't real questions. They were challenges.

A colleague stopped by my office, shutting the door before sitting down. She was someone I trusted, someone who understood both the spoken and unspoken rules of corporate survival.

"Amna," she said, lowering her voice slightly. "There's talk that you're moving too fast. Some people think we should be more... careful."

I exhaled slowly, setting down my coffee. "More careful," I repeated, tilting my head slightly. "What does that even mean?"

She hesitated.

"They just mean... maybe we should ease into this. Get more buy-in before making big changes."

Buy-in. The corporate synonym for stalling.

I leaned back in my chair, measuring my words carefully. "Let me ask you something," I said. "If we had more time, if we played it safe and took fewer risks, do you honestly believe this programme would succeed?"

She hesitated.

"Be honest," I pressed.

Her silence was the answer.

"Exactly," I said. "If this was working, we wouldn't be in this mess to begin with. Playing safe isn't a strategy. It's a slow-motion failure."

She sighed, glancing toward the door as if making sure no one could hear. "I get it. But you know how this place works. Some people—important people—don't like feeling like they're losing control."

I nodded. Of course, they didn't. But here's what people don't understand: The biggest risk is not making a wrong move. The biggest risk is doing nothing. Because in a game where everything is changing, standing still is the fastest way to lose.

So, I had a choice.

Backtrack and soften the message. Or double down and prove why this was the only way forward.

I chose the latter.

Resistance is not always loud. It doesn't always come in the form of outright defiance or aggressive opposition. No, the most dangerous resistance is subtle. It shows up as polite emails questioning whether the changes are "scalable." It takes the form of senior leaders who nod in agreement during meetings but quietly raise concerns in closed-door conversations. It emerges in the whispers of people who feel unsettled by the speed of transformation, who worry that if the game changes too quickly, they might no longer know how to play.

In moments like these, most leaders make the same mistake: They assume that logic will win. They believe that if they present a well-reasoned argument, if they show the data proving that the new approach is working, resistance will dissolve. But logic does not dismantle fear. And fear was at the root of this pushback—not a fear of failure, but a fear of losing control.

I needed to handle this carefully. Push too hard and I risked turning scepticism into outright resistance. Move too cautiously and we'd lose momentum, allowing hesitation to creep back into the cracks we had just sealed. The answer was reframing the conversation as an evolution that everyone had a stake in shaping.

So, I did something that felt counterintuitive. Instead of defending our changes, I called a meeting with the same senior executives who were quietly questioning them. But I didn't walk in with a PowerPoint presentation filled with statistics proving our progress. I didn't list all the reasons why the new approach was the right one. Instead, I did something much simpler.

I put the old system—the one we had dismantled—back in front of them.

On the whiteboard, I sketched out the original project plan, complete with the outdated timelines, the bloated reporting structures, the rigid approval processes that had slowed everything down. Then, I took a step back and faced the room.

"This is what we were working with before," I said, my voice calm but firm. "If we hadn't changed course, where do you think we'd be right now?"

There was a pause. The kind that carries weight.

I let the silence stretch, watching their expressions shift.

"Would we be ahead of schedule? More efficient? Closer to our goals?"

No one spoke. Because the answer was obvious. The old system had been failing long before we changed it. And now, seeing it laid out so plainly, they couldn't argue otherwise.

Then, I turned to the new structure—the one we had implemented. The one they were now quietly questioning.

"I understand the concerns," I continued. "Change feels risky. But I need you to consider this—what's riskier?

Sticking to a plan we already know doesn't work, or re-fining a system that is actually producing results?"

This was the turning point. Because suddenly, the resistance wasn't about the new system being untested. It was about the fact that the old system had already failed and no one wanted to admit how long they had been propping it up.

People don't like to confront the reality that they have been part of a broken system. But once you hold up a mirror, once you force them to see the contrast between what was and what could be, they start to shift.

The meeting ended differently than it began. They still had questions, but now, they were engaged in the solution rather than resisting it. Instead of pushing back against change, they were starting to shape it themselves. And that was the real key—making them feel like this transformation was something they owned, not something being forced upon them. Making them feel like they had a hand in where we were headed. Because they did.

But not all resistance came from leadership. Some of it came from the teams themselves, from the people who had been working under the old system for years and had built their careers around understanding how to navigate its complexities. For them, the fear wasn't about losing control—it was about losing relevance.

I saw it in the way some managers hesitated before making decisions, in the way certain teams struggled to let go of old workflows that no longer served them. These weren't people who were opposed to progress. They were people who had spent years learning how to survive in a rigid, hierarchical environment and now, suddenly, the rules had changed. And when the rules change, people wonder whether they still matter.

The worst thing I could do was dismiss their concerns or tell them to "just adapt." That's not how people work. So instead, I made it clear: this wasn't about eliminating their expertise. It was about elevating it.

"Your value isn't in how well you follow old processes," I told them in one of our team meetings. "Your value is in how well you solve problems, how well you lead through uncertainty, how well you innovate. Those are the skills that matter now."

Then, I did something else. I gave them ownership over the transition.

Instead of dictating every aspect of the new system, I asked them: "What do you think needs to change next? Where do you see friction points? What would make this work better?"

And just like that, the resistance began to shift. Because suddenly, they weren't reacting to change—they were creating it.

This is something most leaders get wrong. They assume that resistance means opposition, when in reality, resistance often just means uncertainty. People aren't rejecting change outright—they just don't know where they fit in once the change happens. Show them their place in the new reality, give them agency, and most will embrace it.

After that meeting, something strange happened. The resistance started to fade. Senior leadership stopped questioning every move. The teams started adapting faster. People who had been sceptical a week ago were now advocating for the new approach. Not because the problems had disappeared overnight. But because they had been given a new way to see them.

And once you change the way someone sees the game? You change the way they play it.

Fear and resistance aren't logical forces. You can present people with all the data in the world, but if they feel threatened—if they believe they're about to lose something—logic won't move them. What will? Perspective.

One of the most powerful tools we used to get people unstuck was something I called the *Perspective Shift*

Wheel. It was a simple visual model divided into four quadrants, each representing a different way to look at any challenge:

1. *Fear:* The instinctive reaction—what's at risk? What could go wrong?
2. *Reality*: The actual, unfiltered truth—what's happening without exaggeration or avoidance?
3. *Opportunity*: The hidden advantage—what does this challenge make possible that wasn't possible before?
4. *Action:* The practical step forward—what's the next move that breaks paralysis?

I introduced it in a tense meeting where a department lead was adamant that scrapping outdated approval steps was reckless. "If we remove these checks," he argued, "we expose ourselves to risk."

I walked up to the whiteboard and divided it into four sections.

"Let's break this down," I said. "Right now, you're here." I tapped the **Fear** quadrant.

- **Fear:** "We'll lose control if we remove these checks."
- **Reality:** "We already don't have control. The delays are causing bigger failures elsewhere."

- **Opportunity:** "If we eliminate redundant checks, we free up compliance teams to focus on high-risk approvals instead of wasting time on routine ones."
- **Action:** "Test a phased rollout—start small, prove the benefits, then scale up."

I turned back to the room. "So, the real question isn't *what if we fail?* It's *what happens if we don't try?*"

Silence. Then, a slow nod. And just like that, the conversation shifted from fear to problem-solving.

We used the Perspective Shift Wheel across multiple teams and each time, it did the same thing: It forced people to detach from their initial emotional reaction and see the challenge as something they could navigate, not something they had to fear.

Because fear only thrives in a vacuum. The moment you put structure around it, the moment you force it into perspective, it loses its grip.

And that's the difference between people who stay stuck and those who rewrite the game.

The First Small Win – Momentum Over Perfection

The moment that proved we were on the right path didn't come with a grand announcement. It came quietly.

A project manager from one of the global teams sent an email:

"Just wanted to flag that since we eliminated the outdated reports, our team has had more time to focus on real issues. We actually solved a bottleneck that's been a problem for months."

It was a small thing. But small things become big things. Because when people see that change isn't just theory—when they experience it in real time—they stop fearing it. They start believing in it. And belief? That's the real tipping point.

There's something fascinating about the way people change their minds. It rarely happens in a single moment. It happens incrementally. At first, people resist. They push back. They argue. Then, they start questioning their own resistance. And finally, they take ownership of the idea as if it had been theirs all along. Once that happens, you've won. Because now, the momentum is no longer coming from you. It's coming from them.

By the end of that first month, we had done something few thought was possible. We had taken a programme that was on the verge of collapse and turned it into something that was actually moving. Not perfectly. Not smoothly. But forward. And that was all that mattered. Because in a game where most people are waiting for certainty before they act, the ones who act first are the ones who create certainty. This was just the beginning. The real work was still ahead. But now? We had proof. Proof that rewriting the game wasn't just an idea. It was a strategy. And it was working.

What Did We Really Do?

Change always sounds elegant in theory. In books and boardrooms, it is framed as a natural evolution, a shift that happens when good ideas meet the right conditions. But in reality, change is messy, uncomfortable, and rarely welcomed. It is one thing to secure buy-in at the leadership level, to have nodding heads in a meeting room when you present a strategy that challenges the status quo. It is another thing entirely to implement that change in the daily grind, where habits and inertia fight against new ways of working. I had spent enough time in corporate environments to know that most transformations fail, not because the ideas were flawed, but because the execution was weak. That meant if this pro-gramme was going to survive, we couldn't just tell peo-ple to adopt a new mindset; we had to create systems that made it impossible for them to operate in the old one.

The moment I stepped out of that critical meeting, where we had torn apart the old project roadmap and declared the end of outdated metrics, I knew the real challenge was just beginning. Change was now an expectation, far removed from what it had been before: a mere concept. But expectations mean nothing without reinforcement. The team was watching, waiting to see if this shift would truly take hold or if it would fizzle out like every other failed attempt at innovation. And I knew how this worked: People default to what feels safe and if given the chance, they would revert to old habits. So, we needed structural reinforcements, mechanisms that would force action even when doubt, fear, or inertia crept in. Change had to become the path of least resistance. And that meant creating three critical systems that would make progress inevitable.

The first battle we had to fight was against wasted time and indecision, the twin killers of momentum. I had seen entire projects collapse because people spent more time talking about problems than solving them. Meetings be-came performance theatre—teams gathered to discuss updates that could have been summarised in an email, leaders postured to signal authority and at the end of it all, no real decisions were made. I had no patience for it. If we were truly serious about changing the way we worked, then the way we communicated had to change first. That led to the introduction of the 15-minute stand-up meeting, a daily ritual designed to strip away unnecessary discussion and force immediate action.

The rules were simple: *No PowerPoint decks. No over-explaining. No reports bloated with vague "progress up-dates."*

Every team member had exactly three things to answer: *What did you accomplish yesterday? What are you working on today? What's blocking progress?* That was it. No more hiding behind bureaucratic jargon. No more waiting for permission to make decisions. Every morning, in fifteen minutes or less, each team had to confront the reality of their own momentum—or lack thereof.

As expected, resistance came immediately. "We need more time to go in-depth," some argued. "There are too many complexities to summarise in such a short meeting," others complained. But within the first week, the shift was undeniable. Issues that used to take days to surface were now exposed in real time. Teams no longer wasted an entire week preparing for ineffective status reports—they had to face their own roadblocks daily, forcing quicker resolutions. The most striking change wasn't in the speed of decision-making but in the accountability it created. When you have to stand in front of your team every morning and declare, "This is what I did yesterday," you start making sure you actually have something to show. There's no place for passive participation in a system like that. You either move, or you expose yourself as someone who isn't pulling their weight. The stand-ups made us own our progress.

But meetings were only one part of the problem. The second battle we had to fight was against fear and secrecy, the silent forces that cripple teams from the inside. The more complex an organisation becomes, the more people start hoarding information, protecting their own domain like it's a private kingdom. Some do it to maintain control, believing that the less others know, the more indispensable they become. Others do it out of fear—fear that if people saw the real numbers, the real failures, the real gaps, they would lose credibility. The result? An environment where people only shared safe, filtered information, never revealing the actual challenges holding them back. If we were going to move fast, if we were going to truly embrace adaptability, we had to destroy that culture of guarded half-truths. Transparency had to become non-negotiable.

To enforce this, we created an open-access progress dashboard, a living document that everyone on the programme could see. Every major decision, every delay, every risk—it all lived in one place, visible to everyone. No more guessing games. No more misinformation. If a project was behind, the team couldn't hide behind ambiguous status reports; the numbers were there in black and white. If an issue was unresolved, it was flagged in real-time for immediate attention. I remember the first time we pulled up the dashboard in a leadership review. There was a moment of discomfort, the kind that comes when people realise they can no longer manipulate the narrative. Someone in the back of the room shifted in their chair, clearly uneasy with the bluntness of the data in front of them. "But won't this make us look bad?" one manager finally asked, hesitant. I didn't hesitate. "It already looks bad," I said. "The difference is, now we can actually do something about it."

At first, the fear was palpable. No one likes to feel exposed. But then, something remarkable happened. The more we forced transparency, the faster problems got solved. Instead of people spending hours drafting elaborate justifications for why something was delayed, they simply addressed it and moved on. Instead of waiting for approval on every small decision, teams started taking ownership, making real-time adjustments because they finally understood how their work connected to the bigger picture. Fear thrives in silence, but when we dragged it into the light, it lost its power.

The third and final battle was the hardest: breaking the old belief that failure was unacceptable. I had seen how perfectionism crippled organisations, how entire teams wasted weeks obsessing over details that didn't matter, afraid to move until they had a flawless solution. That mindset had to die. Progress wasn't about getting everything right the first time—it was about moving fast, learning, and adjusting. So, we implemented a new mantra across every level of the programme: Make decisions quickly, even if they're messy. Course-correct later. But do not stand still. It wasn't enough to say it—we had to prove we meant it. That meant celebrating fast, scrappy problem-solving instead of punishing every minor mistake. It meant shifting performance reviews away from outdated metrics and instead asking: *Did you take action? Did you adjust when needed? Did you keep moving?* The people who thrived in this new system weren't the ones who played it safe. They were the ones who made bold decisions and adapted in real-time.

Looking back, these three systems—the daily stand-ups, the transparency dashboard, and the bias for action— were what saved this programme. They weren't just tools; they were enforcers of the new reality we had built.

They made backsliding into old habits impossible. People didn't just believe in change. They had to live it.

And that was the real victory. Not a perfectly executed plan, not flawless execution. But momentum—real, undeniable momentum. The kind that turns doubters into believers. The kind that separates theoretical success from actual success. The kind that proves that change isn't about what people say they want. It's about what they are forced to do differently every single day.

And in the end, that is the only change that truly lasts.

The Difference

The difference between projects that fail and those that succeed isn't just in the solutions they implement—it's in the questions they ask before they implement them. Too often, we assume we know the cause of a problem and rush toward fixing it, only to realise later that we've been addressing the symptoms rather than the disease. That's why one of the most effective tools we introduced into the programme wasn't a new workflow or a fancy technology—it was a deceptively simple questioning framework called the *5 Whys Technique.*

The concept is straightforward: instead of accepting the first explanation for a problem, you ask *"Why?"* five times in succession, each time drilling deeper into the issue until you arrive at its root cause. This prevents surface-level fixes and forces teams to tackle what's really holding them back.

I remember the first time we applied it in real time. A regional team flagged an ongoing issue—delays in supplier approvals were slowing down an entire phase of the rollout. At first glance, it seemed like an administrative bottleneck. But instead of immediately brainstorming workarounds, we applied the 5 Whys:

1. **Why are supplier approvals delayed?**

    → Because the compliance team is taking longer than expected to review documents.

2. **Why is compliance taking longer?**

    → Because they have a backlog of requests and limited staff.

3. **Why is there a backlog?**

    → Because the system requires redundant manual checks that slow down approvals.

4. **Why haven't we automated these checks?**

    → Because the system wasn't designed to handle high-volume processing.

5. Why wasn't the system built for scalability?

→ Because when it was designed, no one anticipated the complexity of our expansion.

The real issue wasn't compliance delays—it was that we were trying to scale with a system never designed for scale. Without this exercise, we might have pressured the compliance team to "work faster" when what they truly needed was an upgraded infrastructure. Once we had clarity, the solution became clear: automate key approval processes and introduce risk-based reviews instead of applying the same level of scrutiny to every request.

Within weeks, the backlog dropped, approvals moved faster, and what had once seemed like an insurmountable delay turned out to be a fixable design flaw.

We started using the 5 Whys everywhere, and the results were consistent: the deeper you dig, the more you realise that the original "problem" isn't the problem at all. Most organisations stay stuck because they mistake visible symptoms for actual causes. But when you force yourself to ask why—again and again—you begin to see the patterns underneath, the ones that determine whether your efforts will truly create change or just shift the problem elsewhere.

Shifting Perspectives

By the six-month mark, it was clear that we had passed the point of no return. The new way of working had not only taken root—it had become the default. The processes we had once struggled to implement were now second nature. The fear that had initially accompanied every bold decision had faded into something else entirely: confidence.

I saw it in the way meetings unfolded. People spoke with a certainty that hadn't existed before, their suggestions sharper, their willingness to challenge outdated norms more pronounced. The hesitations, the nervous glances at leadership for approval—gone. Instead, decisions were being made without permission, not recklessly, but with the assurance that those making them had the authority to do so. And that was the real shift.

Because the greatest success of this transformation wasn't just that we had changed the way the programme functioned. It was that we had changed how people saw themselves within it.

This is the part of leadership no one talks about enough. The systems, the structures, the strategic decisions— those are important. But the real work? The real, lasting impact? It happens in the minds of the people involved.

Lesson #1: Small Wins Create Irreversible Change

People always look for one defining moment—the single breakthrough that shifts everything. But in reality, big transformations aren't made in sweeping, cinematic moments. They are made in the accumulation of small, almost invisible victories.

It wasn't the grand strategy meetings that cemented our success. It was the daily stand-ups where blockers were cleared in minutes instead of weeks. It was the moment someone realised they didn't need three layers of approval to solve a problem—they could just fix it. It was the day someone took ownership of a challenge not because they were told to, but because it was the natural thing to do.

People didn't wake up one morning and suddenly believe in the new system. They believed in it because they had experienced its benefits firsthand, over and over, until the old way no longer made sense.

And once that happens—once people have *lived* the difference—there's no going back. You cannot convince someone to return to inefficiency once they have felt the power of agility. You cannot force people to accept bureaucracy when they have tasted autonomy. Change, when done right, becomes self-sustaining.

70

Lesson #2: People Don't Fear Change, They Fear Losing Relevance

One of the biggest myths about resistance is that people simply dislike change. That's not true. People are constantly adapting in their personal lives—learning new technologies, shifting careers, adjusting to different environments. Change itself isn't the problem. The real fear is becoming obsolete in the new system.

Some of the loudest resistance had come from the people who had spent years mastering the old game. They weren't fighting against progress; they were fighting against the possibility that they might not have a place in the new world we were building. And that is a different battle entirely.

The solution wasn't to push them aside. It was to show them their value in the new system. To redefine expertise—not as knowledge of outdated processes, but as adaptability, problem-solving, and leadership. The moment they saw that their skills were still essential—just applied differently—the fear evaporated.

And when that happened? They became the fiercest advocates for change.

Lesson #3: Success is a Mindset Shift Before It's a Structural One

Looking back, the most fundamental shift wasn't in how we structured teams or redefined processes. It was in how people thought about success.

Previously, success had been measured by compliance: *Did we meet the deadlines? Did we follow the predefined steps? Did we minimise visible risk?* But that mindset had kept the programme in a state of stagnation, where people were more concerned with avoiding failure than creating progress.

The new success metrics?

- Speed of learning, not speed of execution. If something wasn't working, did we recognise it quickly and pivot?
- Adaptability over perfection. Did we build resilience into our approach instead of forcing rigid plans to fit unpredictable realities?
- Momentum over certainty. Were we moving, experimenting, evolving, instead of waiting for perfect conditions?

These weren't just theoretical ideas. They were practical shifts that changed the way decisions were made. And when success was redefined, everything changed.

Because truthfully, people will always rise to the standard they believe defines winning. If success is about playing it safe, people will do the minimum required to avoid scrutiny. But if success is about taking ownership, about moving boldly, about making things better even when it's risky—people will find a way to embody that.

And they did.

The Final Test - When the Outside World Took Notice

By the time we had completed our first major milestone under this new structure, the transformation was undeniable. The programme—once deemed unfixable—was now being used as an example across the company. Other departments were asking how they could implement similar shifts. Senior leadership, once sceptical, was now fully on board.

At the start of this journey, I thought the hardest part would be changing the system. It wasn't. The hardest part was changing how people saw themselves. People who had once followed instructions without question were now leaders of their own decisions. People who had once been afraid to challenge the process were now the ones refining it. People who had once waited for permission were now acting first, asking later.

And me?

I had walked into this role doubting whether I was ready.

I walked out knowing that readiness is a myth.

Because no one is ready for the biggest moments of their career. No one feels fully qualified for the kind of responsibility that changes the course of an organisation. No one stands at the edge of uncertainty and thinks, *Yes, I have every answer I need.*

But that's the difference between those who lead and those who don't.

The ones who rewrite the game aren't the ones who wait until they feel ready. They are the ones who move forward anyway.

And that?

That's how you win.

The principles in this chapter aren't just for corporate transformation. They apply to every aspect of life and career growth. The moment you stop waiting for permission, the moment you question the assumptions that keep you stagnant—that's when everything changes.

So, now it's your turn.

If you're reading this, there's likely something in your life—a career move, a project, a personal goal—that feels impossible to crack. Something where you've been following rules that no longer serve you. Maybe it's a belief that you need more experience before you're "ready." Maybe it's a process you've been following because that's how it's always been done. Or maybe it's an expectation that's been placed on you that no longer fits who you are becoming.

Whatever it is, challenge it.

Here's your exercise:

1. Identify the Rule You're Following – What assumption, belief, or process are you stuck in? What "rules" are keeping you from progress? Write it down.
2. Use the 5 Whys Technique – Why does this rule exist? Keep asking "Why?" until you uncover whether it's a real limitation or just an outdated belief.
3. Apply the Perspective Shift Wheel – Move through Fear, Reality, Opportunity, and Action. What's actually stopping you? What's the hidden advantage? What's the next move?
4. Rewrite the Rule – If you weren't bound by past expectations, what's the smarter way forward? What would you do differently if no one was stopping you?

And finally, commit to a single bold action this week. A tangible move that breaks the pattern. Because in the end, the people who create real change—whether in businesses, industries, or personal growth—aren't the ones who wait.

They're the ones who rewrite the win.

CHAPTER 3

GROWTH IN DISCOMFORT

———•◦◇◦•———

The room was cold, but it wasn't the air-conditioning. It was the silence. Not the kind of silence that comes from stillness, but the kind that weighs heavy—a silence that indicates something is wrong. No one wanted to be the first to speak because they understood what it would cost them if they did.

At the heart of the discussion sat a name—a real person, someone who had no idea their fate was being decided in this room. They weren't present to defend themselves. They had no idea what was unfolding behind closed doors. And that, more than anything, made my stomach turn.

I watched the small, unspoken cues of unease: A compliance officer tapped a pen against the table—quick, rhythmic, nervous. Someone exhaled too sharply, then glanced down, as if embarrassed by the sound. A manager shifted in his seat, fingers gripping the edge of the table, knuckles white.

No one was comfortable with this. But no one was speaking up, either.

At the head of the table, the figure leading the conversation remained calm, composed, unreadable. No raised voice. No dramatic threats. They didn't need to. Power is rarely loud. It doesn't demand obedience—it expects it. And what was being proposed? It wasn't just flawed. It was deliberate. A quiet decision to cut someone out, to shift blame, to sacrifice a person who wasn't even there to defend themselves.

I knew how this worked. Silence wouldn't make me neutral—it would make me responsible. If I said nothing, I wasn't just allowing it—I was enabling it.

In my mind, a Quranic verse echoed: "O you who believe, stand firm for justice, even against your own selves..." (Surah An-Nisa 4:135).

The right thing to do was clear. That wasn't the problem. The problem was what doing the right thing would cost—reputation, relationships, opportunities that might never come again. I had been in these rooms before. I had learned the unspoken rules—when to nod, when to speak, and most importantly, when to stay quiet.

Challenging a decision like this wasn't just about principle. It was about power. And I knew the moment I opened my mouth, I would be stepping onto the wrong side of it.

I hesitated. Would my voice even carry weight? Would anyone back me? Or would I be left standing alone, knowing that by speaking, I could be *deciding* my own fate?

And then, the thought that changed everything:

"If I stay silent, I am complicit."

Silence wasn't neutral. Silence was permission. And if I stayed silent now, I would be making a choice—a choice to betray my own values.

I believed then, as I do now, that no loss can come from standing for what is right. Yes, I would feel the consequences—being sidelined, shut out, dismissed. But if I stayed silent, the real loss would be far greater. Because if I let fear silence me, what did I truly stand for?

The moment the words left my mouth, the room changed.

Not in volume. Not in loud, obvious outrage. But in something worse. Energy. A flicker of movement. A tightening of a jaw. A glance exchanged between two others, sharp and knowing. A deliberate pause—not long enough to be dramatic, but just long enough to signal what had happened.

I had stepped outside the lines. I had done what wasn't expected of me. And the response? Controlled. Dismissive.

A signal to move on. A polite nod. A vague acknowledgment. A quick return to the agenda. A clear message, wrapped in civility but razor-sharp underneath:

"You just made a mistake."

I scanned the room, searching for even the smallest flicker of support. But the faces that met mine remained neutral. Some turned away, pretending to be focused on their notes. I understood why. But that didn't make it easier to accept.

And the decision?

Temporarily paused.

A brief stall—enough to create the illusion of reconsideration, but without any real chance of the right course of action being taken. I knew it then—I hadn't stopped it. But I had planted a seed.

In that moment, my voice didn't stop the decision.

It didn't turn the tide. But I knew one thing for certain—truth always finds a way.

I had done what I could. Now, the outcome was beyond me.

"When you have decided, then rely upon Allah. Indeed, Allah loves those who rely upon Him"

(Surah Al-Imran 3:159).

I had spoken. I had stood firm. And now, I would trust that the rest was in Allah's hands. Because the easy thing would have been to let it go. To stay quiet. To not draw attention to myself. But that wasn't an option. Because if I had done that—if I had ignored everything in me that knew this was wrong, then who would I have become?

And if I truly believed that justice comes from Allah, then how could I ever believe that standing for it could bring me harm? I may not have seen the results in that moment. But deep down, I knew one thing:

Doing the right thing can never truly harm you. The universe—Allah Himself—will always find a way to balance the scales. And if that was true, then I would do it all again. Without hesitation. I walked out of that room knowing one thing:

I had spoken when it mattered. And in the end, that's the only kind of victory that truly lasts. Because no matter how high the cost, the cost of staying silent is always greater.

I didn't realise it then, but that moment wasn't just about integrity—it was about transformation. The discomfort of that choice wasn't a punishment; it was the first step toward learning the greatest lesson of my career: growth comes from standing firm in the moments that test you the most.

And yet, this is exactly why so many people avoid these moments. Not because they don't know what's right, but because they fear what discomfort will cost them. But what if discomfort wasn't something to escape, but something to embrace? What if it was the key to becoming stronger, not weaker?

Why Most People Stay Silent

People don't stay silent because they don't know what's right. They stay silent because they know exactly what will happen if they speak up. We like to believe that courage is rewarded, that truth has its own power, that justice prevails simply because it should. But in practice, power systems are not designed to reward dissent. They are designed to eliminate it.

Not by silencing people outright—that would be too crude, too obvious. But by making the cost of speaking up high enough that most people will choose self-preservation instead.

The real reason people don't challenge authority is not because they lack principles. It's because they understand the price of resistance. For some, the price is a lost promotion. For others, it's the slow erosion of credibility. For many, it's a gradual diminishing of influence—not fired, not demoted, just systematically sidelined until they barely exist in the spaces where decisions are made.

This is why injustice survives.

I understood, in that moment more than ever, why most people nod along. Because it's easier. Because it's safer. Because it allows you to stay inside the walls of comfort and security. But I also understood something else—something that would define every decision I made from this point forward. If you let fear dictate your choices, you will spend your entire life building a prison out of your own silence.

There is a breaking point for everyone. A moment when you realise that the cost of staying silent is greater than the cost of speaking up.

For me, that moment came in waves. It came when I watched people who had once been vocal slowly train themselves into quiet compliance. When I saw what happened to those who chose comfort over courage—not in one dramatic moment, but in a series of tiny, almost imperceptible compromises.

Most people don't wake up one day and decide to abandon their principles. But silence isn't always a conscious choice—it happens gradually. One overlooked truth at a time. One moment of self-preservation at a time. And sometimes, the cost of speaking up is too high. But when the moment comes where silence feels like a greater betrayal than the risk of speaking out—that's when everything changes.

That's when you realise that power isn't about control. It's about who controls who. And when you stop fearing the consequences of speaking the truth? You take that power back.

This is the heart of *tawakkul*—trusting that the outcome belongs to Allah, even when the path is steep, even when your voice feels small. *Tawakkul* doesn't mean expecting ease because rarely is ease ever present to accept. It means stepping into the fire, knowing Who ultimately carries you through it.

Where True Confidence Comes From

People misunderstand confidence. They think it's about self-assurance, about always knowing the right thing to say, about walking into a room with an unshakable sense of certainty. But real confidence? It's about knowing that even when you're wrong, even when you misstep, even when you face resistance, you will still stand. It's about knowing that your worth is not dictated by how easily you fit in, but by how unwilling you are to shrink.

The world tries to convince us that confidence is loudness, that it is the absence of doubt, that it is the ability to dominate. But the greatest leaders don't lead because they are the loudest. They lead because they know when to speak and when to listen. Because they observe. Because they understand that power does not belong to those who demand it the loudest—it belongs to those who command respect through action.

True confidence isn't about ego. It's about being secure enough to acknowledge your limitations while trusting your ability to make decisions despite uncertainty. And this is where most people struggle—because we've been conditioned to see confidence and humility as opposites, when in reality, the strongest leaders hold both.

Nelson Mandela was one of the most formidable leaders of the 20th century. After spending nearly three decades in prison, he emerged not bitter, not vengeful, but measured, strategic, and deeply attuned to the complexities of leadership. He exuded confidence—not the chest-thumping, ego-driven kind, but the quiet, unwavering confidence of someone who had endured suffering and emerged unbreakable. And yet, Mandela was also known for his humility. He listened. He learned. He never assumed he was the smartest person in the room. He understood that his power was not just in his ability to command but in his ability to unite.

This ability to hold confidence and humility at the same time is a learned skill. A mindset. And yet, most people fail to develop it because they believe leadership is about dominance rather than adaptability.

Steve Jobs, for all his reputation as a visionary, was known for changing his mind completely when presented with better arguments. He was confident in his ability to create game-changing products, but he was not arrogant enough to believe he always had the right answers. He surrounded himself with brilliant people, not to affirm his ideas, but to challenge them. And that ability—to push forward when necessary but pivot when needed—is what allowed him to build a company that redefined technology.

This is where most people fail. They become too attached to being right. They mistake confidence for stubbornness. They assume that admitting they were wrong is a sign of weakness, rather than a sign of growth. But the reality is, the people who succeed in the long run are not the ones who are always right. They are the ones who are always willing to learn.

Because confidence without humility leads to arrogance—a refusal to evolve, a resistance to feedback, an insistence on protecting ego at all costs. But humility without confidence leads to paralysis—self-doubt that prevents action, a constant seeking of external validation, and an inability to trust your own judgment.

The key is knowing when to activate each one.

⬥ When to trust yourself and when to listen.

⬥ When to move forward with conviction and when to pause and reassess.

⬥ When to assert your position and when to acknowledge that someone else may have a better perspective.

True confidence is not the absence of doubt. It is the ability to keep moving forward, even when doubt exists. And true humility is not self-deprecation. It is the ability to recognise that you will always have more to learn.

The greatest leaders, the most successful individuals, the people who leave a lasting impact on the world are not those who fit neatly into one category or the other. They are those who understand that real power, real wisdom, real success—lies in the balance between the two.

True confidence isn't about playing by existing rules. It's about knowing when the rules themselves are flawed. The greatest leaders, the ones who transform industries and rewrite history, don't just trust themselves—they trust their ability to see what others don't. And sometimes, that means breaking the rules that hold everyone else back.

When the Playbook Stands in Your Way

There is a certain comfort in following the rules. They offer structure, predictability, and a roadmap that promises, at least in theory, a pathway to success. From the moment we enter the education system, we are taught to follow instructions, respect hierarchy and operate within the expectations that have already been established. The message is clear: If you work hard, if you do what you're told, if you follow the playbook exactly as written, you will succeed.

But what happens when the playbook itself is flawed? What happens when the existing rules were not designed for innovation but for preservation? What happens when the very structure that promises stability is the same one keeping you stuck?

The truth is, most systems are not built to create success. They are built to control it. They are designed to maintain order, not to foster breakthrough thinking. And the people who succeed in the most extraordinary ways—the ones who redefine industries, change the course of history, or revolutionise the way we think—are not the ones who blindly follow the rules. They are the ones who recognise when the rules are the problem.

But breaking the rules is not about rebellion for the sake of rebellion. It is not about recklessly discarding structure or defying authority simply to make a statement. The most effective disruptors, the people who create lasting change, do not break rules indiscriminately—they break them strategically and with full awareness of why they must be broken.

There is a reason why the Wright brothers were the ones to crack the code of human flight when the greatest engineering minds of their time had failed. At the dawn of aviation, the world's most respected scientists were convinced that the key to flight was sheer power—that if they could build an engine strong enough, a plane would take to the sky. And so, they kept making bigger engines, heavier machines, more forceful thrust systems. And they kept failing.

The Wright brothers, however, had no formal training in engineering. They had no prestigious funding, no access to the resources of world-renowned institutions. But what they did have was the ability to question assumptions. They didn't accept that flight was about power—they focused on control. They studied birds. They tested aerodynamics instead of obsessing over engines. While everyone else was focused on force, they were focused on balance.

And when they succeeded, when their fragile, lightweight craft lifted off the ground at Kitty Hawk in 1903, it wasn't because they had better resources. It was because they had ignored the playbook.

The same pattern repeats across history.

Most people never reach that level of thinking because they are waiting for permission. They believe that if an idea is truly valuable, it will be recognised. That if a system is truly flawed, someone will eventually change it. That if a rule is truly meant to be broken, an authority figure will come along and authorise the breaking of it.

Why Most People Stay Stuck

The greatest obstacle to challenging the rules is not external—it is internal. It is the deeply ingrained belief that authority must know best. It is the conditioning that tells us that if something has been done a certain way for years, there must be a reason. It is the fear of stepping outside the lines, of risking failure, of becoming the one who speaks up when no one else will.

There is a fascinating psychological study known as the Asch Conformity Experiment. Participants were shown a series of lines of varying lengths and asked to identify which ones matched. The task was simple. The answer was obvious. But here's the twist—each participant was placed in a group where everyone else was secretly in on the experiment.

One by one, the group members—who were all actors— began to give the wrong answers. They did this with complete confidence, as if the incorrect choice was un- questionably right. And what happened? The real partic- ipants, despite knowing the correct answer, began to doubt themselves. They started to second-guess their perception, hesitating before making a choice. Some even went along with the wrong answers simply because everyone else did.

Why?

Because going against the group feels uncomfortable. Because we are wired to believe that if everyone else is doing something a certain way, they must know some- thing we don't.

This is the same force that keeps people stuck in jobs they hate, in systems that don't serve them, in routines that no longer make sense. It is not because they are in-capable of change—it is because they fear being the only one to make the move.

One thing is certain.

Every major breakthrough, every system that has ever been revolutionised, every institution that has ever been disrupted, began with someone who was willing to be the only one. Someone who was willing to look at an entire room of people nodding along and say, "This doesn't make sense." Someone who was willing to challenge the assumptions that everyone else accepted as truth. Some-one who was willing to stand at the edge of uncertainty and move forward anyway.

The key to breaking the right rules is about learning how to ask better questions.

The next time you find yourself blindly following a rule, a process, a convention, ask yourself:

- Who created this rule? Was it designed for effi-ciency, or was it created to serve an outdated model of thinking?
- What would happen if this rule didn't exist? Would progress stop? Or would it actually accel-erate?

- Who benefits from this rule staying in place? Is it designed to serve people, or is it designed to serve systems that are no longer relevant?
- What is the risk of breaking this rule? Is the risk real, or is it just a fear of stepping outside what's familiar?

Because here's the reality: The people who change the world are not the ones who wait for permission. They are the ones who see what is broken and have the courage to fix it. The question is—will you be one of them?

This fear of breaking the rules, of stepping outside the known, is what keeps most people stuck. But history—and psychology—tell us something different. Growth, real transformation, doesn't come from safety. It comes from facing discomfort head-on. In fact, researchers have found that some of the most significant growth doesn't just come from small challenges, but from life's biggest adversities.

Discomfort + Reflection = Transformation

Growth does not happen in comfort. This is one of those truths that everyone hears, everyone nods along to, but very few people fully absorb. It's easy to agree with the idea in theory—yes, challenges make us stronger, failure is a learning opportunity, struggle builds character. But when discomfort becomes real— when it's no longer an abstract principle but something that is pressing down on your chest, tightening your throat, making you question everything about yourself—that's when most people retreat.

Because discomfort does not feel like growth. It feels like uncertainty. It feels like doubt. It feels like failure. And failure? That is the thing most people spend their entire lives trying to avoid. But the mistake isn't in fearing discomfort. The mistake is in misinterpreting what discomfort actually means.

The problem is that our brains are wired to avoid pain. This is not weakness—it's biology. The human mind has a built-in negativity bias, an evolutionary survival mechanism that prioritises risk avoidance over progress. Thousands of years ago, this made sense. Avoiding uncertainty meant avoiding actual danger—wandering too far from familiar terrain could lead to predators, consuming an unknown food could be deadly, challenging authority in a primitive society could result in exile, which was effectively a death sentence.

But today?

Today, our fear responses have not evolved at the same pace as our environment. The same ancient wiring that once kept us alive now prevents us from taking necessary risks. The same mental reflex that once warned our ancestors not to enter dangerous territory now whispers to modern humans, "Don't apply for that job. You'll get rejected." "Don't start that business. It might fail." "Don't speak up in that meeting. You'll embarrass yourself."

And so, we stay in our comfort zones.

We mistake familiarity for security and stability for progress.

We tell ourselves that avoiding discomfort is the same as avoiding failure, when in reality, avoiding discomfort is failure—because it means we never even tried.

Now, I want you to follow closely.

The most successful, resilient, and extraordinary people are not the ones who never experience discomfort. They are the ones who learn how to sit with it.

There is an entire field of psychological research dedicated to the idea that adversity, when processed correctly, can be a powerful catalyst for transformation.

It's called post-traumatic growth.

Most people are familiar with post-traumatic stress disorder (PTSD), where a deeply distressing experience can leave a person stuck in cycles of fear, anxiety, and avoidance. But researchers have found that, for some, adversity takes a different path. While trauma can leave lasting scars, in certain cases, individuals experience a different phenomenon—post-traumatic growth.

They actually emerge stronger.

They report feeling more resilient, more adaptable, more appreciative of life. They describe seeing new possibilities they had never considered before. Their sense of purpose intensifies—they become less concerned with trivial worries and more focused on what truly matters.

This phenomenon is known as *post-traumatic growth (PTG)* and it highlights a powerful truth: While trauma can leave deep scars, *not all difficult experiences result in long-term suffering.*

So, what makes the difference?

Processing.

Discomfort alone is not enough. Suffering without reflection is just suffering. Pain, when left unexamined, is nothing but an open wound. But when you pause, analyse, extract lessons, and consciously apply them to your future decisions, you don't just recover—you transform.

This is why two people can go through similar adversity but emerge with completely different outcomes.

For some, the experience **remains unresolved**—not by choice, but because trauma is complex and healing isn't linear. Others, however, can process their pain in a way that fuels growth. They sit with the discomfort, but instead of avoiding it, they reflect on it: *What did this teach me? Where did I go wrong? What should I do differently next time?* They take the lessons and use them as fuel to become someone new.

Some of the most resilient, successful individuals in history had catastrophic failures before they achieved anything remarkable.

- Oprah Winfrey was demoted from her first television anchor job because she was told she was "too emotional" for TV.
- J.K. Rowling was rejected by twelve publishers before someone finally gave Harry Potter a chance.

Had they allowed their first failures to define them, they would have faded into obscurity. But they didn't.

Instead, they used failure as information.

They asked themselves:

- What did this experience teach me?
- How can I use this setback as data rather than a verdict?

- Where do I need to grow before I try again?

And then they got back to work.

The Moment of Choice

Right now, there is something in your life that feels uncomfortable.

A conversation you're avoiding.

A risk you're hesitating to take.

A decision you know you need to make, but fear is keeping you frozen.

Ask yourself:

Is this discomfort a sign that I should retreat? Or is it a sign that I'm about to grow?

Because more often than not, the moments that feel impossible today are the stories of growth you'll tell tomorrow.

And the only difference between those who evolve and those who don't?

One group embraces discomfort.

The other avoids it.

Which one will you be?

If you want to take this further—if you want to ensure that you are always learning, always growing, always evolving—start keeping a Growth Ledger.

Here's how:

Step 1: Identify Three Moments of Discomfort
Think back to three times in your life when you were forced into discomfort. These could be challenges at work, difficult conversations, major life decisions—anything that pushed you outside your comfort zone.

Step 2: Extract the Lesson
For each moment, write down:

- What was the hardest part?
- How did you respond?
- What did you learn from it?

Step 3: Apply It Forward
Now, think about a challenge you're facing right now. What lesson from your past experiences can you apply to this moment?

You've already survived difficult things before. You've already proven that you can adapt, grow, and rise beyond what you thought was possible. And that means you can do it again.

In the end, the real test of growth isn't what you do when it's easy. It's what you do when the room is silent—when every instinct tells you to stay small. Because those moments don't just shape decisions. They shape identity. And if you can stand firm, even when the cost is high, you don't just change yourself. You change the room.

CHAPTER 4

WHEN THE GAME IS RIGGED, BUILD YOUR OWN

——•◦◇◦•——

I had done everything right. I had followed the formula—take on responsibilities beyond my role, deliver results under pressure, and make myself indispensable. I had played the game exactly the way it was supposed to be played. And for a while, I believed that was enough. I believed that if I just stayed on course, if I pushed harder, if I continued proving my worth, then when the time came—when promotions were decided, when leadership opportunities were handed out—my name would be on that list.

It wasn't arrogance. It wasn't entitlement. It was confidence built on tangible proof: the long nights spent fixing problems I hadn't created, the quiet sacrifices of my personal time to meet deadlines, the recognition from colleagues who turned to me when things got complicated because they knew I could handle it. I had stacked up reason after reason for why I had earned my place. So, when the email came in—when the list of names was announced—I expected, at the very least, to be among them.

I scrolled through the names once. Then again. A slow, creeping sensation settled into my stomach, something between disbelief and a quiet, simmering rage. My name wasn't there.

I sat there, staring at the screen, the words blurring slightly as my mind raced through possible explanations. Maybe it was an error. Maybe they hadn't finished finalising the list. Maybe there was some mistake in the way it had been communicated. I wanted to believe there was another explanation. That maybe I had missed something. That maybe I wasn't as visible as I thought. That maybe, despite the long nights, the extra effort, the results that spoke for themselves—I just wasn't good enough.

The self-questioning crept in slowly, then all at once.

I wish I could say I rose above it effortlessly. But the truth is, the doubts weren't just whispers—they were shouts. Every setback echoed with a question: Was I fighting a battle I could never win? Was I attempting to rewrite rules that were never meant to include me? There were days I questioned everything, replaying meetings in my mind, wondering if I had been too bold, too asssertive, too... different. But every doubt, every second-guess, built a quiet resilience. I realised that if I was going to rewrite the rules, I had to be willing to lose the game they wanted me to play.

Was I working hard enough?

Was I making the right connections?

Had I overlooked some unspoken rule, some nuance I hadn't picked up on?

I replayed the decisions that had led me here, the sacrifices I had made, the moments I had gone beyond what was expected—only to be met with silence. Maybe I had miscalculated. Maybe I had overestimated my value. Maybe I had convinced myself I was indispensable when, in reality, I was just... replaceable.

That thought lingered longer than I'd like to admit. The quiet fear that maybe I had simply asked for too much, that I had expected the system to recognise me when it had never been designed to.

And then, something shifted.

I remembered the names on that list—the people who *had* been chosen. I thought about the way they moved, the way they fit effortlessly into spaces that had always

104

been made for them. I thought about the meetings they walked into with ease, the quiet confidence they carried, the way opportunities found them rather than the other way around.

And that was when the self-doubt cracked. Because I knew, without a shadow of a doubt, that it wasn't about competence. It was about visibility. About presence. About access to the spaces where decisions were made. They moved through the company with an ease I couldn't replicate. Unspoken biases didn't announce themselves. They lived in the moments of hesitation, the quick glances exchanged when I entered the room, the surprise when I spoke with authority. But they also gave me an advantage. I learned to read people before they even spoke. I became hyper-aware of body language, of the power dynamics shifting with each word spoken. It was survival at first. But then, it became strategy. I turned their underestimation into my advantage—by the time they realised I was a threat to the status quo, I was already two moves ahead.

They had a familiarity with leadership that wasn't earned through performance but inherited through unspoken social bonds. They came from the same backgrounds, shared the same inside jokes, attended the same out-of-office gatherings where real decisions were made. They didn't have to prove themselves over and over. They were assumed to be competent. Assumed to be leadership material. Assumed to be the future of the company.

And then there was me.

As a young, female, Muslim in a space where leadership often looked the same, my presence was already a statement. I didn't just walk into rooms—I disrupted the unspoken expectation of who should be there. My identity wasn't just a part of me; it was a lens through which every action, every word, was interpreted. It meant that assertiveness could be mistaken for defiance, that ambition could be perceived as audacity. It meant that before I even spoke, assumptions were being made. This wasn't just about breaking stereotypes—it was about navigating a reality where I was seen before I was heard.

The first time it happened, I told myself I was imagining it.

I was in a meeting, offering a solution to a problem we had been circling for weeks. I laid it out clearly—concise, actionable, directly tied to the business goals. The moment I finished, there was a brief silence. And then, as if I hadn't spoken at all, someone else—someone who had been in the Friday night conversations—repeated my point.

This time, it landed.

Nods of agreement. A comment about how insightful it was. A decision to move forward with it, as though it had just been introduced for the first time. I sat there, stunned. Not because I hadn't seen it happen before, but because it had just happened *to me*.

The first instinct was to let it go. To convince myself that maybe I hadn't phrased it quite right, that maybe I should have been more assertive, that maybe this was just how things worked. But the more I paid attention, the more I saw it wasn't just me. It was a pattern. One I wasn't willing to let continue.

So, I started pushing back.

I stopped letting my ideas dissolve into the room, waiting to be picked up by someone else. If I saw my point being recycled, I interrupted. If I wasn't given space, I created it—leaning forward, speaking with intent, making eye contact with the decision-makers so there was no room to pretend I hadn't contributed.

I was young and youth in professional spaces often reads as inexperience. I was a woman and that alone was enough to make me an outlier in a leadership pool that still skewed overwhelmingly male. I was visibly Muslim, which meant that before I even opened my mouth, I was marked as different. And the worst part? It wasn't outright discrimination. It wasn't anything I could point to and say, "There—this is the moment I was held back." That would have been easier. What I was facing was something more insidious. Something woven into the fabric of how workplaces function.

The Pub: Where Careers Are Made

Every Friday afternoon, a quiet shift would take place. There was no official announcement, no reminder emails, no formal gathering—just an unspoken understanding. Laptops were shut a little earlier, jackets were thrown over shoulders, and a steady migration of colleagues made their way out of the office, all heading in the same direction: the pub. It wasn't a policy. It wasn't mandatory. But if you wanted to be in the loop, if you wanted to be seen, if you wanted to move ahead, this was where you had to be.

At first, I thought it was just socialising—a harmless, end-of-week ritual for blowing off steam. But the more I observed, the more I realised that this was something else entirely. This was where relationships were built, where casual conversations turned into career opportunities, where people let their guard down and in doing so, formed the kind of connections that would carry them forward. The following week, someone who had been at the pub on Friday night would suddenly be included in a high-profile project. A role that had never been formally posted would be quietly filled by someone who had been "in the conversation." By Monday morning, decisions had already been made—decisions I had never even known were up for discussion.

I watched it unfold from the sidelines, aware that I was missing something but unwilling—or unable—to fully step in. It wasn't about the drinking. That was the easy explanation, the surface-level excuse. But the truth ran deeper. I could have ordered an orange juice, could have stood at the edge of the group, could have tried to blend in. But the real problem wasn't the alcohol. It was the feeling of not belonging, the quiet but unmistakable awareness that I was an outsider in a space where familiarity was currency. The laughter that came easily to them felt forced when I tried to participate. The references, the inside jokes, the cultural shorthand—it all felt like a language I wasn't fluent in.

So, every Friday, I stayed behind. At first, I told myself it didn't matter. That I wasn't missing much. That my work would speak for itself. But then Monday mornings would come, and I would overhear snippets of conversation, fragments of decisions that had already been made. A new initiative, a reshuffling of responsibilities, a promotion that had seemingly materialised out of nowhere. Except it hadn't. It had been decided in those few hours I wasn't there.

I told myself it wasn't personal. That these were just co-incidences. That if I kept my head down and focused on delivering results, my work would be enough. But the evidence was undeniable. The ones who advanced weren't always the best performers. They were the ones who were seen. Who were remembered. Who were familiar. And I wasn't.

I started questioning everything. Maybe I was being paranoid. Maybe I was imagining the connections that weren't really there. Maybe I was looking for an excuse, a reason why I wasn't progressing as quickly as I had expected. But then I started paying closer attention, and the patterns became impossible to ignore.

It wasn't just the pub. It was the side conversations at coffee breaks, where new ideas were tested before being formally pitched. It was the client dinners where relationships were forged, where alliances were built before negotiations even took place. It was the way people gravitated toward those they already knew, those they already trusted, those who looked and sounded like them. And it was the way decisions—real, career-defining decisions—were made long before any official announcement.

I still remember the Monday morning when it became crystal clear. I walked into the office expecting the usual team meeting, but the air in the room was different. Conversations were already flowing, people were nodding at each other knowingly, a sense of excitement crackling in the air. I sat down, listening closely, trying to piece together what had happened. And then I heard it—a new project was kicking off. A major one. The kind that could make someone's career.

I glanced at my manager, waiting for my name to come up. It didn't. Instead, it went to someone who, as far as I knew, had no particular experience in that area. I was still trying to make sense of it when I overheard a casual remark exchanged between two colleagues.

"Yeah, we were talking about it on Friday night... seemed like a great fit, so we thought—why not?"

That was it. That was the moment it all sank in.

I hadn't just missed an opportunity. I had never even been in the running. Not because I wasn't qualified. Not because I hadn't put in the work. But because, when the conversation that mattered took place, I hadn't been in the room.

And that's when I knew—the game wasn't rigged against me specifically. It was just designed for those who already belonged.

The Reality of Religious Practices in High-Pressure Workplaces

It was just another workday for everyone else. Another morning coffee in hand, another lunch meeting scheduled, another afternoon energy slump remedied with a quick snack. But for me, it was different. I sat through the same meetings, handled the same deadlines, engaged in those high-pressure conversations—but without food, without water, and without any sign that it was affecting me. Because it couldn't affect me. There was no adjustment made, no recognition of the endurance required to function at full capacity while fasting.

There's something deeply isolating about fasting in an environment where no one else is. Not because of hunger or thirst—those were expected, those were manageable—but because of the subtle, unspoken ways it made me feel like I was operating in a completely different world. While others grabbed quick bites between calls, I sat still. While colleagues perked up after their afternoon coffee, I had to push through the exhaustion that settled in around midday, keeping my focus sharp despite the sluggish pull of an empty stomach and dry throat. And yet, the expectations remained exactly the same.

It wasn't that people were inconsiderate. Most just didn't notice. It didn't cross their minds that, while they were running on caffeine and full meals, I was running on sheer willpower. That while their energy dipped and surged throughout the day, mine only declined—steadily, persistently, testing the limits of my mental and physical endurance.

And still, unlike in countries where fasting is widely observed, where workdays are shortened or adjusted to accommodate the physical toll, here, nothing changed. There were no alternative working arrangements, no allowances for reduced hours, no quiet acknowledgment that those fasting might need to move differently. Meetings were scheduled as usual. Workloads remained heavy. The pace never slowed.

I had learned, early on, that bringing it up—asking for accommodations, even something as small as shifting a meeting to a time when I wouldn't be at my lowest—risked being seen as an inconvenience. There was always that quiet fear in the back of my mind: *Would they think I'm less capable? Would they assume I'm not strong enough to handle the pressure? Would it be used, even unconsciously, as a mark against me when promotions or leadership decisions were made? Would it cause anyone to unintentionally look down on my faith, something I would never accept?*

So, I endured in silence. I sat in boardrooms, my mouth dry, my hands clasped under the table to hide any slight tremor from dehydration. I spoke with measured precision, careful not to let my voice betray the fatigue creeping in. I remained sharp, composed and unwavering—because in spaces where you already have to work twice as hard to be taken seriously, there is no room for visible struggle.

The hardest part wasn't the physical discomfort. It was the fact that no one else had to think about this. No one else had to consider how their performance might subtly decline under these conditions, or how their commitment to their faith might inadvertently become a liability in a corporate environment that thrives on an unspoken expectation of sameness.

And yet, despite the exhaustion, despite the quiet barriers that no one else saw, I never let it diminish my impact. Because, just like every other invisible challenge, I knew the solution wasn't to seek recognition—it was to keep proving, over and over, that I could perform at my highest level, even when the odds were stacked against me.

"Life will test you, but remember, when you walk up a mountain, your legs get stronger."

The Moment I Stopped Waiting for Permission

That was the hardest part to accept. That I had spent so much time waiting. Waiting for someone to recognise my effort. Waiting for an opportunity to present itself. Waiting to be invited in. It was almost embarrassing to admit how long I had spent hoping that if I just did good work, that would be enough. But it wasn't. The game didn't work that way.

So, I stopped waiting.

I didn't announce it. There was no grand declaration, no dramatic moment of rebellion. Just a quiet, internal shift. A decision. If I wasn't going to be included, then I would have to change the way I played. I wasn't going to become someone I wasn't—I wasn't suddenly going to start forcing myself into after-work drinks or laugh at jokes I didn't find funny or try to squeeze myself into spaces where I felt like an outsider. But I was going to make sure that when I spoke, people listened. That when I contributed, it wasn't just background noise. That I didn't just take up space—I owned it.

"Nothing ever goes away until it has taught us what we need to know."

It started small.

115

I learned to be comfortable with silence. I had spent years feeling like I needed to prove myself in every meeting, to over-explain my ideas, to justify my decisions before anyone even challenged them. But I started watching the people who had power, the ones who were listened to without effort. They didn't rush to fill silences. They didn't ramble. They spoke with certainty, they let their words settle, they commanded attention by the weight of their presence, not just their volume. So, I practiced. I started saying less, but making sure that when I did speak, it mattered.

It felt unnatural at first, resisting the urge to over-explain, to fill the space. But something interesting happened. People started paying more attention. When I wasn't always the first to speak, my words carried more weight when I finally did. And more than that—I felt a shift within myself. I no longer felt the need to prove that I belonged. I already knew that I did.

But mastering the room was only part of the equation. Influence wasn't just about presence—it was about access. And if I couldn't access the informal circles where power was exchanged, I had to create my own.

I stopped wasting time trying to win over people who had already decided I wasn't part of their world. Instead, I started seeking out the ones who actually valued results over image, the ones who made decisions based on competence, not camaraderie. I found mentors—not the ones who were the most visible, not the ones who were the loudest, but the ones who actually got things done. The ones who were respected because of their knowledge, their execution, their ability to move things forward.

I didn't try to charm them. I didn't try to "network" in the traditional sense. I just made myself indispensable. I learned to anticipate problems before they happened, to offer solutions before I was asked, to make their jobs easier in a way that they couldn't ignore. And over time, without me ever needing to be in the pub on a Friday night, without me needing to force myself into places where I didn't belong, I built my own version of influence. One based not on being liked, but on being needed.

But perhaps the most powerful shift—the one that changed everything—was realising that even if I couldn't be in the room, my ideas could be.

If there was one skill that changed my trajectory more than anything else, it was writing. Not the kind of writing that was meant to impress, not the kind of writing that was flowery or complex or filled with unnecessary words. The kind of writing that was impossible to ignore. Every email, every report, every document I produced became a tool of influence. I didn't just write to communicate—I wrote to shape decisions. I made sure that my insights weren't just observations, but that they framed the conversation in a way that made my perspective indispensable.

At first, it was subtle. I noticed that when I wrote something down, people started repeating it in meetings, as if the idea had taken on a life of its own. Then, I saw that even when I wasn't in the room, my perspective was being referenced. Eventually, people started coming to me—not because I had forced my way into their circles, but because they realised that I had something valuable to contribute.

It was a quiet kind of influence, one that didn't require me to change who I was, one that didn't require me to chase validation from people who had never planned to give it to me. And over time, it did something else—it freed me.

I remember walking into those rooms, feeling the weight of expectations that weren't just about my skills but about everything I represented. I was the outsider, the one who wasn't supposed to be there. I tried to play their game, to fit into spaces that were never designed for someone like me. But every time I moulded myself to their rules, I lost a piece of who I was.

It took me years to realise that I didn't have to play their game—I could create my own. I could lead not by imitating them but by leaning into my own strengths, by embracing everything that made me different. And when I did that, when I stopped trying to fit into their boxes, I found a power I never knew I had.

I stopped apologising for taking up space. I stopped hesitating when someone spoke over me in a meeting. I stopped softening my words to make them more palatable. I stopped deferring, stopped waiting, stopped looking for permission. And most of all, I stopped trying to downplay the parts of me that made others uncomfortable.

I had spent too much time explaining myself. Why I didn't drink, why I needed time to pray, why I wouldn't be at certain social events. But at some point, I realised—I didn't need to explain. I didn't need to ask for understanding. I didn't need to make myself smaller so that others could be more comfortable. I had let myself believe, for far too long, that success required assimilation. That the price of moving forward was blending in.

But the truth was, the more I owned who I was, the stronger I became.

There was power in not asking for permission. Power in refusing to contort myself into something I wasn't.

Power in recognising that if the spaces I was in didn't accept me, I had every right to create my own. And once I made that shift—once I stopped seeking validation from a system that was never built for me—I stopped feeling like an outsider. I wasn't on the sidelines anymore.

There's a quiet kind of heartbreak that comes with realising the door you were knocking on will never open for you. The kind that doesn't announce itself with devastation but settles in like a dull ache—a recognition that no matter how hard you try, some spaces were never meant to include you.

But there's also a quiet kind of freedom in letting go of what was never meant for you.

It took me a long time to see it that way. To shift from *Why wasn't I chosen?* to *Maybe this wasn't my path to begin with.*

And that's where *tawakkul* changed everything.

Tawakkul is faith in Allah even when you don't understand His plan.

Even when the rejection stings.

Even when the setback feels unfair.

120

Even when every logical part of you believes this was the path you were supposed to take.

There's a reason we don't always get what we think we want. Because sometimes, the thing we're chasing isn't meant to elevate us—it's meant to limit us. And sometimes, the thing we see as an obstacle is actually redirection to something better.

I stopped seeing rejection as a failure. I started seeing it as an answer.

If the door wouldn't open, I wasn't going to stand outside waiting.

And in that shift, I found something stronger than success. I found certainty—not in the outcome, but in the belief that what was meant for me would never miss me.

I was in control.

The Quiet Victory: Winning on My Own Terms

The game was never designed to be fair. Not in the workplace, not in business, not in the unwritten rules of who gets ahead and who gets left behind. For too long, we're taught that success is a straightforward equation: work hard, deliver results, prove yourself. But if that were true,

the most talented, most hardworking, most capable people would always rise to the top. And we know that's not
what happens. The promotions go to the ones who are
seen, the opportunities go to the ones who are heard, and
the decisions are made long before the official conversations begin.

This is where most people get stuck. They either accept
the game as it is, resigning themselves to the idea that
they'll never fully fit in, or they exhaust themselves trying to play by rules that were never written for them in
the first place. But there's another way. A way that
doesn't require you to beg for a seat at the table, to force
yourself into spaces where you don't belong, or to mould
yourself into something more palatable just to be accepted.

Success isn't just about working hard. It's about posi-
tioning yourself so that your work cannot be ignored. It's
about creating influence in ways that don't require permission. It's about understanding that visibility isn't
vanity—it's necessity. The people who move forward
are not always the most skilled or the most deserving;
they are the ones who have learned how to make themselves undeniable. And the moment you stop waiting for
someone to give you access, the moment you stop playing by a set of rules designed to keep you one step behind, you start to see the cracks in the system.

And that's where you begin to rewrite the rules.

Take a step back. Look at the spaces where influence is built in your world. Where are the side conversations happening? Who is making the real decisions, and where are those decisions being made? Maybe it's not a pub on a Friday night. Maybe it's a closed-door meeting. A golf course. A text thread you're not on. A private Slack channel. A casual mention over lunch. Wherever it is, ask yourself: how can I create my own version of that? How can I insert myself into the spaces that actually matter, in ways that don't require me to change who I am?

The shift begins when you stop thinking of yourself as someone who needs to be included and start operating as someone who holds power—regardless of whether you are given recognition for it. If you cannot be in the room, make sure your work speaks so loudly that it enters without you. If you are not part of the conversation, position yourself as the person whose insight is necessary before any real decisions can be made. If you are being overlooked, make yourself so valuable that even the most biased of systems cannot ignore you. This isn't about learning how to conform. It's about learning how to move differently.

So, here's your challenge. Take a hard look at where you are right now and ask yourself: *What is the invisible barrier keeping me from where I want to be? What spaces am I waiting to be invited into? And how can I stop waiting and start creating my own leverage?*

Then, take one action today that shifts the dynamic in your favour. Maybe it's writing something that shapes a key decision. Maybe it's building relationships with the people who actually move the needle, rather than the ones who are simply loudest. Maybe it's refusing to shrink the next time someone talks over you in a meeting. Maybe it's finally acknowledging that you are done waiting.

Because the game will never be fair. But once you realise you don't need fairness to win—just strategy—everything changes. If the game is rigged, stop playing by their rules. Build your own strategy—and win your way.

Everything that made me feel like an outsider was actually my greatest advantage. Every time I was excluded, every time I was overlooked, every time I was made to feel like I didn't belong—it forced me to find another way. It sharpened my ability to see through the noise, to spot the real levers of power, to move with precision rather than force. And eventually, it made me unstoppable.

That is the real lesson. The world makes space for people who refuse to wait for permission. The ones who step forward, who stop explaining, who take action before they feel ready. The ones who decide, without hesitation, that they will shape their own success on their own terms.

Now, the only question is—what will you do?

CHAPTER 5

THE BREAKING POINT

BEFORE THE BREAKTHROUGH

———•◇•———

"And sometimes life is just hard, and some days are just rough... and sometimes you've got to cry before you can move forward. (And all of that is okay.)"

Kristan Higgins

There comes a moment in life—sometimes slow and creeping, other times sudden and brutal—when everything starts to collapse. The ground beneath you shifts, the air around you tightens, and no matter how much you struggle, it feels like you're drowning in a world that refuses to slow down. The chaos is relentless. It doesn't wait for you to gather your thoughts or pause for you to catch your breath. You're

126

left grasping at fragments of certainty, trying to piece together a plan while the walls cave in around you.

It's a peculiar thing, the way chaos takes over. It doesn't announce itself with the kind of clarity that demands immediate action. It seeps in quietly, first as a minor inconvenience, then as a dull, persistent hum of anxiety, until one day, you wake up feeling like a stranger in your own life. You move through the motions, but there's no sense of control—just an exhausting loop of doubt, pressure and expectations you can't seem to meet.

The truth about breaking points is that they don't feel like transformation in the moment. They feel like failure. The moment your mind unravels, the second your body gives up, the instant you realise you've run out of solutions— it doesn't feel like the beginning of something new. It feels like the end of something you've spent years trying to hold together.

No one talks enough about this part—the space between what was and what could be. The in-between, where clarity feels out of reach and doubt settles in like a familiar companion. You can have people who care about you. People who love you. People who want to help. And yet, during the storm, you are alone.

Not because they don't want to be there for you. But because they can't feel what you feel. They see the exhaustion, the stress written in the tension of your shoulders, the restless energy that keeps you awake at night. They offer solutions, encouragement, even distraction. But they don't see the part of you that feels like it's disappearing. They don't see how heavy it is to carry the weight of uncertainty every single day.

And so, even when they try, even when they mean well, they can't reach the part of you that feels lost. That's the hardest part of chaos.

But what if the unravelling isn't the problem? What if the breaking point is just the moment before a breakthrough?

There was a time when I thought I had mastered control. I knew how to plan, how to anticipate, how to manoeuvre through challenges with precision. Life, to me, was a game of calculated moves—strategy over spontaneity, execution over uncertainty. I thrived in environments where I could outthink my problems, solve my way through setbacks, and emerge stronger on the other side.

Until one day, I couldn't.

It wasn't a single catastrophic event that knocked me down. That's the thing about real chaos—it rarely arrives in the form of one big, cinematic disaster. It sneaks in through a series of small, seemingly insignificant moments, each one eroding your confidence, your energy, your ability to think clearly. And then, suddenly, you're at the bottom of a hole you don't remember falling into.

I remember waking up one morning, my body heavy with exhaustion despite getting more sleep than usual. There was a fog in my head, a strange kind of mental static that made it impossible to think clearly. Simple decisions felt monumental. Tasks that once came easily felt overwhelming. I tried to push through it, convinced that I just needed to work harder, focus more, regain control.

But the harder I pushed, the worse it got.

I found myself staring at my laptop screen for hours, unable to form a single coherent thought. Deadlines loomed, messages piled up, and yet I sat frozen—paralysed not by laziness or procrastination, but by something deeper. Something heavier. I had spent years relying on my ability to think fast, to make decisions under pressure, to find solutions where others saw dead ends. And yet, here I was, unable to function in the very role I had built my identity around.

I was supposed to have it all figured out. People looked to me for answers, for stability, for solutions. And I had spent so long playing that role—being the one people relied on, the one who had it together, the one who could

129

always find a way forward—that I started to believe the same thing.

Until one day, I couldn't. And the moment I realised I was lost, the moment I knew I was unravelling, the worst part wasn't just the fear. It was the fact that no one else could see it.

Because when people expect you to be strong, they don't always notice when you start to break. They assume you'll figure it out, that you'll find a way through, that you'll keep holding everything together like you always have. And so, you learn to suffer in silence, convincing yourself that asking for help would only make things worse.

After all, if you don't have the answers, who will?

That's the thing about being the one others rely on. No one realises you need saving, too.

The worst part wasn't the exhaustion or the mental fog. It was the fear. The fear that I had lost something essential. That I had burned out my ability to perform, to think, to lead. The fear that I would never find my way back to the person I used to be.

It began with hesitation. Not the thoughtful pause of someone searching for the right words, but the kind of silence that traps the words before they can form. I would open my mouth, knowing exactly what I wanted to say, but somewhere between my mind and my voice, the connection broke. Nothing emerged.

At first, I dismissed it. Maybe I was just tired. Maybe my mind was processing too much at once. But then it happened again. And again. Simple conversations—answering an email, giving a quick response, explaining an idea—became impossible hurdles. I could hear the words in my head, could feel their weight, but the moment I tried to speak them, they slipped away, like fog dissipating before I could catch it.

I had spent my life believing that my mind was my greatest tool—my ability to think fast, articulate clearly, solve problems on the spot. And suddenly, that tool was failing me. I wasn't just tired. I wasn't just distracted. I was unravelling in a way I didn't know how to fix.

That was the moment I knew—this wasn't just stress. This was something deeper. Something that wasn't going to disappear with a good night's sleep or a weekend off. My mind, my voice, my very sense of self—they were slipping away.

And I didn't know how to get them back.

I tried to explain it, but how do you articulate something you don't even understand yourself? How do you tell someone, "I feel like I'm falling apart," when everything on the outside looks fine? How do you admit, "I don't know how to fix this," when you're the person others rely on for solutions?

That's the silent weight of chaos. It isolates you. It convinces you that no one else will understand, that asking for help is weakness, that slowing down is failure. And so, you grip tighter. You tell yourself to push harder. You refuse to let go, even as everything around you—and within you—begins to collapse.

The Reality of Chaos - Why We Struggle with Uncertainty

Chaos doesn't just disrupt our lives—it disrupts our minds. It shakes the very foundation of how we process the world. We like to think we're rational beings, capable of assessing situations calmly and making strategic decisions under pressure. But when faced with real uncertainty—when life hands us an unexpected crisis, when the future becomes foggy, when everything we thought was certain suddenly unravels—our brains react in ways we don't always understand.

The truth is, chaos overwhelms us because we are wired to resist it. The human brain is an efficiency machine, built for pattern recognition and predictive thinking. We crave stability because stability means survival. Our ancestors didn't have the luxury of thriving in ambiguity—uncertainty meant danger. A rustle in the bushes could mean a predator, an unfamiliar landscape could mean losing your way. Those who hesitated, who second-guessed, who failed to recognise patterns quickly, didn't survive long enough to pass on their genes.

Even now, in our modern world—where there are no sabre-toothed tigers lurking in the shadows—the brain still treats uncertainty as a threat. And when the unknown enters our lives, we don't respond with measured logic. We respond with instinct.

At its core, uncertainty is a psychological blind spot. We struggle with it not because we lack intelligence or resilience, but because our brains are designed to prioritise certainty over ambiguity.

1. The Overwhelm Effect - When Too Many Unknowns Create Mental Paralysis

Have you ever tried to make a decision while standing in the middle of a chaotic room—phones ringing, people talking over each other, information flying at you from every direction? It is almost impossible to focus. Your brain freezes, overloaded by the sheer number of variables it has to process at once.

This is the *Overwhelm Effect* in action.

When faced with too many unknowns—too many moving parts, too many things we can't control—the brain enters a state of cognitive overload. It struggles to prioritise, to filter, to make sense of what's happening. Instead of acting decisively, we shut down. We freeze. We feel stuck, incapable of moving forward because the mental weight of uncertainty is too much to carry.

It's why people delay making big life changes, why they stay in jobs they hate, put off difficult conversations. It's not laziness—it's paralysis. When the path ahead is unclear, taking any step at all feels impossible.

2. The Negativity Bias - Why Our Mind Defaults to Worst-Case Scenarios

The human brain isn't just designed to resist uncertainty—it's designed to assume the worst about it.

Enter the *Negativity Bias*, the psychological tendency to give more weight to negative experiences than positive ones. This bias was another survival mechanism built into our evolutionary hardware. If our ancestors underestimated a threat, the consequences were fatal. But if they overestimated a threat—even if it wasn't real—they stayed alive.

Fast forward to today and this same bias still runs the show.

134

When we face uncertainty, our brain doesn't default to optimism. It doesn't say, *This could turn out great!* Instead, it jumps to worst-case scenarios.

- *What if I fail?*
- *What if I make the wrong decision?*
- *What if everything falls apart?*

It's why we spiral when chaos hits. We don't see uncertainty as neutral—we see it as inherently dangerous. And so, we brace for impact, preparing for the worst, convinced that if we don't control every variable, disaster is inevitable.

The Three Common (But Ineffective) Responses to Chaos

When faced with uncertainty, people tend to fall into one of three instinctive reactions. These responses feel natural, but they don't help—they only deepen the chaos.

Some people respond to uncertainty by ignoring it. They push it aside, convince themselves it's not a big deal, tell themselves, *I'll deal with it later.*

But uncertainty doesn't disappear just because we refuse to acknowledge it. In fact, ignoring chaos only makes it grow. Like an unpaid bill stacking up interest, the problem compounds. By the time it can no longer be ignored, it has already become far more unmanageable than it was in the beginning.

This is how people end up blindsided by crises they "never saw coming." It's not that the signs weren't there—it's that they refused to look at them.

On the opposite end of the spectrum are those who respond to chaos with excessive control. They micromanage, they obsess over details, they refuse to let go of even the smallest variables.

It makes sense—when the world feels unpredictable, control feels like safety. But the problem with over-controlling is that the tighter we grip, the more we crack under the pressure. Life isn't something we can command like a chessboard. It's unpredictable by nature. And when we refuse to accept that, we only exhaust ourselves trying to force order onto something inherently uncontrollable.

The result? Burnout. Frustration. And ultimately, collapse.

The third common response is panic—a frantic attempt to regain control by doing *something, anything,* just to feel like we're taking action.

This is what happens when people make impulsive decisions in a crisis. When they jump into new careers without thinking, end relationships out of fear, or drastically change direction without any real plan. It's not strategy—it's reaction. And more often than not, it only creates more chaos.

Panic doesn't solve problems. It creates new ones.

If avoidance, over-control, and panic don't work, then what does? How do people who thrive in uncertainty manage to do so?

The answer isn't resistance—it's navigation.

When you study individuals who perform under extreme pressure—chess grandmasters, elite military strategists, airline pilots dealing with in-flight turbulence—you notice a pattern. They don't react emotionally to chaos. They don't try to eliminate uncertainty. Instead, they focus on structured navigation.

A chess grandmaster doesn't try to predict all 20 possible moves ahead. They make the best move they can in the present moment. An airline pilot in turbulence doesn't panic or overreact. They adjust altitude, make small, calculated changes, and stay the course. Successful businesses don't cling to failing strategies. They adapt, evolve, and find new opportunities within the uncertainty.

These individuals understand something most people don't: Chaos isn't a crisis. It's an invitation.

It's an open space where reinvention happens. Where growth occurs. Where transformation begins.

The people who navigate chaos successfully aren't necessarily smarter or more prepared. They simply don't resist uncertainty. They move with it, rather than against it.

The C.L.A.R.I.T.Y Framework - A Roadmap Through the Fog

Chaos is both an external force and an internal battle. It's the unpredictable nature of life—financial struggles, unexpected failures, personal losses—but it's also the way we internalise those moments. The way we resist them. The way we convince ourselves that we should be able to outmanoeuvre the storm.

The problem isn't chaos itself. The problem is the expectation that we're supposed to have it all figured out.

We admire those who appear unfazed by uncertainty, who seem to move through life with unwavering confidence. But what we don't see are the moments behind closed doors—the doubts, the breakdowns, the nights spent questioning everything. The truth is, nobody has it

all figured out. Not the CEOs, not the world-class athletes, not the thought leaders who preach resilience from
a stage. Everyone faces the fog. Everyone hits the wall.

But the ones who make it through? They don't fight the
chaos. They navigate it.

And that was the shift I needed to make.

I had spent my entire life believing that clarity was something you achieved *before* making a decision. That certainty was the prerequisite for action. That once I had a
plan, once I had mapped out every possible outcome,
then I could move forward.

But clarity isn't found in endless analysis. It's found in
movement.

That realisation changed everything.

I stopped trying to force control over every detail. I
stopped waiting for the perfect moment to act. I stopped
treating uncertainty as a sign that I was failing. Instead,
I leaned into the unknown. I took one small step, even
when the path ahead was blurred. And then another. And
another.

And somewhere along the way, the fog started to lift.

It's easy to believe that we need all the answers before
we take action, that we need a perfect plan before we

begin. But the truth is, clarity doesn't arrive as an epiphany—it's something we build, step by step, decision by decision.

Every breakthrough begins in the fog.

C – Choose What Matters: Cutting Through the Noise

When you're in the middle of chaos, everything feels urgent. Every problem demands your attention, every option pulls at your mind. Every unfinished task feels like it could be the one thing that makes or breaks your success. But most of it doesn't matter—not in the way you think it does.

If you study the most effective leaders, thinkers, and high performers, you'll notice they have an almost ruthless ability to prioritise what truly matters while ignoring everything else. They don't get trapped in the noise of the moment. They don't chase every loose thread or expend energy on things that won't move the needle.

The problem most people face isn't that they don't work hard enough—it's that they're spread too thin, trying to hold onto everything at once. They treat every fire as a five-alarm emergency, every distraction as something requiring immediate resolution. And in doing so, they lose sight of the one or two things that actually deserve their focus.

At its core, this step is about understanding that not all chaos is created equal. Some of it is nothing more than background noise—loud, distracting and stressful, but ultimately insignificant. Other parts of it contain the decisions, actions, or moments that will define everything. The skill lies in knowing the difference.

I remember a moment in my life when the sheer weight of responsibilities felt unbearable. Deadlines, obligations, expectations—piling up like an avalanche.

My instinct was to tackle everything at once, to believe that I could outwork the chaos if I just tried hard enough. But the harder I pushed, the more paralysed I became. It wasn't until I asked myself one simple question that things became clear:

"If I could only focus on one thing right now, what would make the biggest impact?"

The answer was obvious—but I had been too overwhelmed to see it. I had spent weeks drowning in details that, in the grand scheme of things, wouldn't matter a month from now. I had let distractions masquerade as priorities. But the moment I stripped everything down to one singular focus, the fog lifted. I moved forward. And that single step set off a chain reaction that made everything else easier.

The next time you feel overwhelmed, stop and ask yourself:

"What's the one thing I can focus on that will create the biggest impact?"

Not ten things. Not five. Just one.

Clarity begins with choosing what matters. And choosing what matters begins with the courage to ignore what doesn't.

L – Lessen the Noise: The Art of Strategic Elimination

The world is louder than ever. There were days when I felt like I was being pulled in a thousand different directions, each demand screaming for my attention, each email carrying the weight of someone else's expectations. I remember opening my inbox one morning, seeing 126 unread messages, and feeling my chest tighten. I hadn't even started the day and I was already behind.

I tried to respond to each one, convincing myself that productivity was about clearing the noise. But the more I tried to keep u, the more I lost track of what actually mattered. I was reacting, not choosing. And somewhere in the chaos of everyone else's priorities, I lost sight of my own.

The turning point came when I missed an important deadline because I was buried under tasks that didn't matter. I had prioritised the noise over impact. That was the day I realised: Being busy isn't the same as being effective. And if I didn't learn to filter the noise, I would drown in it. Most of what is stealing your focus is utterly irrelevant. In chaotic times, the temptation is to gather more information, to analyse more variables, to believe that if you just had enough data, you'd make the right decision. But too much input creates paralysis. It muddies the waters instead of clarifying them. The difference between those who navigate chaos effectively and those who drown in it isn't intelligence or luck—it's their ability to shut out unnecessary noise.

The brain has a limited capacity for decision-making. Every moment you spend deliberating over something that doesn't truly matter is energy stolen from the things that do.

In practical terms, this means constantly asking yourself:

- **Is this urgent, or is it important?**
- **Is this something I truly need to deal with, or is it a distraction?**
- **What can I eliminate, delegate, or defer?**

Most people don't struggle because they lack information. They struggle because they're drowning in too much of it.

Take a moment; write down the top three things causing you stress right now. Now look at that list and ask yourself:

- **Which of these actually matters?**
- **Which of these am I holding onto out of habit rather than necessity?**

Then, cross something off. Let it go. The moment you do, you'll realise how much lighter your mind becomes. Clarity isn't found in more—it's found in less.

A – Adapt Rapidly: The Power of Flexibility Over Perfection
There is a myth we love to believe: that the people who succeed are the ones who planned everything perfectly from the start. But perfection is fragile. It cannot withstand reality. But truthfully, most adaptable people are the ones who thrive. They understand that rigid plans break under pressure, while flexible strategies evolve.

History is full of examples of individuals and organisations that failed because they clung too tightly to a plan that no longer worked. They saw the signs that change was necessary but refused to adjust, paralysed by their original vision. And then, there are those who thrive not because they never face chaos—but because they pivot before chaos turns into collapse.

The best entrepreneurs and leaders are not the ones who never encounter setbacks. They are the ones who course-

144

correct quickly. The same principle applies to anything in life. Your plans will break. Your expectations will fail you. But your ability to move with the uncertainty rather than against it is what will determine your outcome.

One of the greatest lessons I ever learned came from a moment when my original plan failed spectacularly. I had mapped out every step. I had accounted for every variable—except for the fact that life doesn't care about your careful calculations. Everything fell apart. And for a moment, I was tempted to grip tighter, to double down on a plan that was clearly broken.

But then, I made a different choice. I pivoted. I let go of my attachment to what was "supposed" to happen and adapted to what was actually happening. That decision didn't just save me—it led to an outcome better than I could have planned.

Ask yourself:

"Am I sticking to this path because it's the best one, or because I'm afraid to change direction?"

There is strength in persistence. But there is wisdom in knowing when to shift. The faster you learn to adapt instead of resist, the smoother your navigation through chaos will be.

R – Reassess and Reframe: The Power of Shifting Perspective

There is a moment in every difficult situation where you are given a choice. You can either let the chaos define you, or you can redefine it on your terms. This is the essence of cognitive reframing—the ability to see the same set of circumstances through a different lens and, in doing so, alter its impact on you. The facts don't change, but the way you interpret them does.

The most successful people don't avoid pressure; they reframe it. What most people see as obstacles, they see as steppingstones. What most people experience as stress, they experience as fuel. The challenge is the same, but the mindset is different.

Take elite athletes, for example. When competing at the highest level, the margin for error is razor thin. The difference between winning and losing often comes down to how an athlete interprets the moment. Some athletes crumble under the weight of expectations, paralysed by the enormity of what's at stake. Others reframe the pressure as an opportunity—a chance to show up, to rise to the occasion, to test their limits.

The same applies to business, relationships, and personal crises. Stress, uncertainty, and failure are all inevitable. What separates those who spiral from those who thrive is their ability to assign meaning to the experience.

146

Imagine you lose a job unexpectedly. The natural reaction is panic—fear about money, career stability, self-worth. But reframing allows you to look at the same situation and see something else: freedom, a reset, a forced but necessary transition into something better. The job loss hasn't changed, but your narrative around it has.

This is where the 5 Whys method becomes invaluable. When you feel stuck, overwhelmed, or defeated, ask yourself five times:

1. Why is this bothering me?
2. Why does that matter?
3. Why am I afraid of that?
4. Why do I believe that fear is valid?
5. Why is this actually an opportunity?

What happens after the third or fourth "why" is a shift—you start uncovering the real reasons behind your stress. And often, the real issue isn't what you thought it was. You aren't afraid of failing the exam—you're afraid of what people will think if you do. You aren't worried about ending a relationship—you're scared of being alone. You aren't hesitant to take a risk—you're terrified of looking foolish if it doesn't work out.

But when you reframe the fear, the uncertainty, the setback, you take its power away. You move from reacting to chaos to redefining it on your own terms. And that changes everything.

I – Implement Incrementally: The Myth of the "Right Time"
One of the biggest myths we tell ourselves is that we need to wait for the perfect moment to act. That clarity must come first. That we must have a detailed plan, a roadmap, an absolute certainty about the outcome before we begin. But clarity doesn't come before action—it comes because of action.

Ryan Holiday writes about the power of small, deliberate movements. Not grand gestures. Not sweeping changes. Just tiny actions, repeated consistently, that create momentum.

The problem most people face isn't that they don't have a plan—it's that they never start. They overthink. They wait for the stars to align. They let uncertainty paralyse them. But if you look at every major breakthrough in history, every great achievement, every significant transformation, it started with a small, seemingly insignificant action.

A writer doesn't wake up one day with a finished manuscript. They sit down and write the first imperfect page. A business doesn't become successful overnight. It starts with the first customer, the first sale, the first attempt.

The key is to break tasks down into their smallest possible steps. This is where the *Two-Minute Rule* becomes so powerful. The idea is simple: If a task feels overwhelming, shrink it until it's so small that you can't fail.

- Instead of saying, "I need to write a book," say, "I'll write 50 words."
- Instead of "I need to get in shape," say, "I'll do five push-ups."
- Instead of "I need to figure out my career," say, "I'll update my resume."

What happens next is almost magical: Once you start, momentum takes over. That first step leads to another. And another. And suddenly, the thing that felt impossible becomes possible—not because you had all the answers upfront, but because you moved anyway.

So, whatever it is that you've been putting off, stop waiting for the right moment. The right moment is the moment you decide to take the first step.

T – Trust the Process: The Paradox of Clarity

There's a paradox when it comes to uncertainty: the more you try to figure everything out before moving, the more stuck you become. Overthinking creates a mental traffic jam where every possibility competes for space, leaving you unable to move in any direction.

This is where the *Zeigarnik Effect* comes into play—a psychological phenomenon that explains why unfinished tasks create mental tension. Your brain doesn't like loose ends. It seeks resolution. And when you start something—even in the smallest way—your mind naturally pushes you forward to complete it.

This is why taking action, even without perfect clarity, is so powerful. But taking that first step felt impossible. I remember staring at my laptop, a blank document mocking me, daring me to write something that mattered. I typed, deleted, rewrote, and deleted again.

Days turned into weeks, and my perfectionism became procrastination. I wasn't waiting for the right moment—I was avoiding the fear of failing. I hit my lowest point one night when I looked at the clock and realised I had spent six hours avoiding the one thing I needed to do. I closed my laptop, feeling defeated and ashamed. But in that moment, I realised that waiting for clarity was costing me my confidence.

So, the next day, I made a decision: I would write one imperfect sentence. Just one. It felt small, almost insignificant, but it was enough to break the paralysis. And once I started, the words began to flow. They weren't perfect but they were real. And that was the moment I understood: Clarity isn't something you wait for. It's something you create. Once you begin, your mind works to find solutions you never would have seen while standing still.

But trusting the process isn't just about psychology—it's about faith.

Tawakkul, in Islam, is the idea that once you've done your part—once you've made the effort, taken the step, done the work—you surrender the outcome to something bigger than yourself. You let go of the obsession with results. You stop gripping so tightly to things you can't control.

Because at some point, you have to move forward without guarantees. You have to accept that uncertainty is part of growth. And you have to remind yourself that certainty isn't a requirement for progress—only movement is.

Y – Yield and Iterate: Knowing When to Let Go

There is a difference between giving up and letting go. One comes from fear; the other comes from wisdom.

One of the most dangerous traps in life is the *Sunk Cost Fallacy*—the tendency to hold onto something simply because you've already invested time, energy, or money into it. People stay in jobs they hate, relationships that drain them, and projects that are clearly failing just because they've already put so much into them.

But past investment doesn't justify future suffering.

The most successful people aren't the ones who stubbornly cling to failing strategies—they are the ones who know when to pivot. When to let go. When to yield to a new direction.

I once made the mistake of holding onto something far too long. A venture that wasn't working. I kept forcing it, sinking more money, more effort, more time into something that had already proven it wasn't the right path. And why? Because I didn't want to admit it had failed.

It took me two years too long to realise that letting go wasn't failure—it was a strategy. And the moment I did, everything changed. Because the energy I had been wasting trying to revive something dead? I channelled it into something new. Something better.

A simple question can change everything: What's the worst that can happen if I walk away?

Most of the time, the answer is far less scary than we imagine.

The goal of this framework—of navigating chaos, of finding clarity—isn't about perfection. It's about movement. One step at a time. One choice at a time. And sometimes, the best move isn't pushing harder—it's stepping back.

Because clarity isn't something you wait for. It's something you create.

Walking Through the Fog

After the struggle, after the exhaustion, after the relentless doubt. You don't always notice it happening. Clarity rarely arrives with trumpets and fanfare. Instead, it comes quietly, like the first light breaking through a heavy fog. One day, without realising when or how, you look up, and the path that once felt impossible to find is right there in front of you.

I remember the exact moment I knew the *C.L.A.R.I.T.Y Framework* worked—not just as an idea, not just as a theory, but as a lifeline. It wasn't during an easy time. It wasn't when things were already improving. It was when everything still felt impossibly uncertain.

I had been fighting a battle with myself, clinging to control, chasing perfection, demanding answers from a universe that wasn't ready to give them. The weight of uncertainty had reached its peak—I had convinced myself that clarity was something external, something I had to find before I could move forward.

But then, something shifted.

Not because the chaos disappeared. Not because a perfect opportunity suddenly materialised. But because I stopped trying to force certainty and instead focused on the next step in front of me.

I chose what mattered. I silenced the noise. I adapted. I reframed. I took small, deliberate actions instead of waiting for a grand revelation. I trusted the process. And most importantly, I let go of what wasn't working. That was the moment everything changed—not because the storm ended, but because I had learned how to move through it.

Tawakkul is faith in Allah, even when you don't understand His plan. Even when everything feels like it's falling apart. Even when your mind tells you there's no way forward.

I had always believed that control was the key to success. That if I planned well enough, worked hard enough, anticipated every outcome, I could outmanoeuvre uncertainty. But when the chaos swallowed me whole, when I lost my sense of direction, I realised something:

I was never in control to begin with. And that realisation—though terrifying at first—became my greatest source of peace. Because if I was never fully in control, then maybe it wasn't my job to hold everything together.

Maybe I wasn't supposed to have all the answers. Maybe my role wasn't to fight the storm, but to trust the One who sees the path even when I can't.

I didn't understand why this was happening. I didn't know when—or if—I would feel like myself again. But for the first time, I stopped gripping so tightly to the illusion of control.

And when I did? The weight lifted. Because *tawakkul* isn't about knowing the way. It's about trusting that the way exists.

The Power of Those Who Stay

When chaos takes over, when exhaustion weighs down every thought, the world feels like it is shrinking around you. The worst part isn't the struggle itself—it's the isolation that comes with it.

People mean well. They want to help. But most don't know how. They offer solutions, advice, encouragement—but none of it lands. None of it reaches the part of you that feels lost inside yourself. And so, most people fade away. Not because they don't care, but because they don't know what to do with someone who isn't "fixable."

But then, there are the ones who stay.

The ones who don't demand explanations. Who don't rush to fill the silence. Who don't expect you to be okay before you're ready. They don't offer solutions because they know there are none. They just stay.

Their presence is the only thing louder than the chaos. Not their words—just their being. They sit beside you, quiet but steady, grounding you when your own mind feels like it's unravelling. They remind you, without needing to say it, that you are still here. That you still matter. That you are still worth waiting for.

And when the fog starts to lift, when you finally take a breath without feeling like you're suffocating, you will look around—and they will still be there. Because they always were.

The storm won't last forever. The clouds will part.

The chaos, the uncertainty, the endless questions—none of it is permanent. But clarity doesn't come from waiting for the storm to pass. It doesn't come from forcing answers before they're ready. It comes from choosing to move, even when you don't feel ready.

And when you do? When you take those first uncertain steps?

One day, you'll look up and realise the fog has lifted. You'll see that the moments that felt unbearable were actually shaping you. That the uncertainty that once paralysed you was actually pushing you toward something better.

And when you reach that moment, you'll understand this truth:

Clarity isn't found in the absence of chaos. It's found in the way we choose to navigate it.

CHAPTER 6

THE CEILING THAT WASN'T A CEILING

———•◇•———

*"The first principle is that you must not fool yourself—
and you are the easiest person to fool."*

Richard Feynman

For as long as I could remember, I had played by the rules. I had done everything I was supposed to do. Hard work, adaptability, relentless pursuit of excellence—these had always been my guiding principles. And for years, they had served me well. Each step forward in my career had felt almost inevitable. There was always a next opportunity, a door that opened just as I was preparing to walk through it. It was never effortless, but it was predictable. If I put in the work, I saw the results. If I faced a setback, I course-corrected, learned from it, and moved forward with even more determination.

But suddenly, all of that changed.

I still remember the exact moment it hit me. It wasn't a dramatic revelation, not the kind you see in movies where the protagonist has an epiphany under flickering streetlights in the rain. It was quieter than that. A slow, creeping realisation that settled in my bones, one that I tried to ignore for months.

I was sitting in front of my laptop, scrolling through job postings that, at one point, would have seemed like a logical next step. But now, I wasn't sure if they even applied to me anymore. Every role I looked at seemed slightly out of reach or strangely unappealing. I adjusted my CV again, tweaking the language, making sure my experience and achievements stood out. I wrote new cover letters, reached out to former colleagues, activated my network. I did everything I had been taught to do. And then—I waited.

And nothing happened.

Weeks passed. Then months. My inbox remained frustratingly empty, except for the occasional automated rejection. The silence was unnerving. I had built my career on momentum—so why had everything ground to a halt?

At first, I told myself it was just a matter of timing. The market was slow. Companies were being cautious. I just needed to be patient. But as time stretched on, the excuses started to sound hollow. The people around me were moving forward. I was still here, trying harder and harder to force doors open that refused to budge.

Then came the whispers. Not from others, but from inside my own mind. The ones that sting because they carry the weight of truth.

"Maybe you're being too picky."

"Maybe your skills aren't as relevant anymore."

"What if you've peaked?"

It was an uncomfortable thought, one I didn't want to entertain. But it lingered. No matter how much I tried to drown it out with logic, it kept resurfacing at the worst moments—late at night, in the pauses between emails, in the silence after a phone call that didn't lead anywhere.

I had spent years teaching leaders how to navigate change, guiding businesses through transformation. And yet, here I was, struggling to recognise my own transformation in real time. I wasn't failing—I was out of alignment.

And if you've ever been in that place—where everything you've built starts to feel disconnected from where you're heading—you know how terrifying it is.

The doubt seeps in. The confidence you once had begins to erode. You question if you're doing something wrong, if you should go back to what's familiar, even if it no longer fits. But growth doesn't allow you to go backward.

We are conditioned to chase success in ways we understand—to pursue the paths that have worked for us before. But what happens when those paths disappear? When no matter how hard you push, the doors that once opened so easily refuse to move?

Most people assume they've hit a dead end. But what if the ceiling you're pressing against isn't a block—what if it's a sign that you were meant to build something entirely new?

I didn't see it at first. I only knew that I was exhausted from pushing against something that refused to move. But I kept trying—because when you've spent a lifetime being rewarded for effort, it's hard to accept that effort alone doesn't create progress.

Then, one day, it hit me. The problem wasn't me. The problem wasn't the job market. The problem wasn't my experience, skills, or value. The problem was that I was trying to succeed using the wrong strategy for the stage I was in.

For years, my focus had been on execution—taking action, solving problems, making things happen. But now, execution alone wasn't enough. I was trying to move forward without first redefining what success actually meant for me.

It was as if I had been aiming at a target that no longer existed. And you can't hit a target you can't see.

That's when everything shifted.

I stopped looking at success as a straight line. Instead, I started to see it as a series of stages, each requiring a different mindset, a different approach. And when I recognised that, everything changed.

The Five Stages of Success Design

The biggest reason people struggle isn't because they lack skill, intelligence, or ambition. It's because they don't recognise what stage they're in. They apply the wrong strategies at the wrong time. They push forward when they should be stepping back for clarity. They hesitate when they should be committing fully. They overthink instead of executing. They give up too soon because they don't recognise that setbacks are part of the process.

That's where the *Five Stages of Success Design* comes in.

Every period of growth—whether it's in your career, business, personal life, or creative pursuits—follows this structure. When you understand what stage you're in, you know what to focus on. You stop wasting effort on things that don't move you forward. You stop feeling lost in the process.

- **Clarity** – This is where it all begins. You step back to define what success actually looks like for you—right now, not based on old goals or external expectations.

- **Commitment** – Once the vision is clear, you decide. Not halfway. Not conditionally. This stage is about alignment and choosing to go all in, even when the path ahead is uncertain.

- **Execution** – Now comes the doing. You take focused, deliberate action. No more procrastinating or perfecting. Progress over perfection.

- **Resilience** – Setbacks will happen. This stage is about staying in the game. Adapting. Learning. And holding onto your direction when things don't go to plan.

- **Integration** – This is the stage most people skip. It's where you pause to reflect, acknowledge your growth, and recalibrate before the next chapter begins. It's how transformation becomes sustainable.

When I looked at my situation through this framework, I realised that I had been operating in execution mode when I actually needed clarity and commitment. I had been trying to force myself into an old definition of success instead of designing a new one. And that was the key. Success isn't about doing more. It's about doing the right thing at the right stage. The moment I understood that, I stopped feeling stuck. I stopped questioning my value. I stopped forcing a version of success that no longer fit me. Because I wasn't supposed to stay where I was. I was supposed to evolve.

And now, you have this framework too. Because no matter where you are—whether you're at the beginning of something new, in the middle of a challenge, or at the edge of reinvention—there's always a way forward.

The question is: Do you know what stage you're in?

Because when you do, everything changes.

Stage 1: Clarity – Defining What Success Looks Like

For years, success had been defined for me—promotions, salary increases, bigger responsibilities, higher stakes. It had always been about *more*. But now, for the first time, that version of success wasn't available to me. And instead of redefining it, I was stuck trying to chase a version of success that no longer fit me.

I was measuring myself against an outdated metric.

I see this happen all the time. Brilliant, capable, hard-working people pushing themselves to exhaustion—not because they aren't good enough, but because they haven't defined what "good enough" even means anymore. They assume that if they just keep going, the picture will become clearer. That effort will eventually create direction.

But that's not how it works.

Clarity doesn't come from movement. It comes from stopping long enough to define the target. And I had never done that before. I had spent my career chasing *progress*. But I had never actually asked myself: *Progress toward what?*

One day, I came across a quote so simple it almost felt ridiculous.

"If you ever feel useless, think about the white pencil."

At first, I laughed. But then, it hit me. A white pencil seems invisible—like it has no purpose. But that's only because it's being measured on white paper. The moment you place it on black paper, its value becomes undeniable. Its usefulness was never the problem. It was just being measured in the wrong context.

That was exactly what I had been doing to myself. I wasn't failing. I wasn't stuck. I wasn't losing value. I had just been measuring my success in the wrong place. The white pencil isn't missing value. It's just missing contrast. And that's when I realised: I needed to redefine my success on my own terms.

Let me ask you:

- Have you actually defined what success looks like for you *now*? Not the version you had five years ago, not the version that others expect, but the one that actually aligns with the life you want today.
- Are you measuring yourself by outdated metrics, like a white pencil trying to prove its worth on white paper?
- If you stripped away job titles, external validation, and what other people think—what would success truly feel like for you?

Because let me tell you this; success isn't lost. It's only ever undefined. And if you don't define it, the world will do it for you. For years, I let external factors dictate what success meant. But when I finally stopped chasing an outdated definition and started defining success in terms of impact, fulfilment and alignment, everything changed.

I stopped feeling like I was running in place. I stopped feeling like I had to prove myself in the wrong spaces. And most importantly, I stopped feeling like I was failing. Because for the first time, I actually knew what I was aiming for.

If you want to break out of the cycle of uncertainty, you have to get clear about what success means to *you*. And that starts with asking three simple questions:

1. What does success look like for you—right now?

Not the version you had five years ago. Not the version that others think you should have. But the one that actually aligns with the life you want to build.

2. How will you know when you've reached it?

If your definition of success is vague, you'll never feel like you're achieving it. What are the tangible markers? How will you measure progress in a way that actually matters?

3. Why does this goal matter to you?

Because if your definition of success is built on what you *think* you should want instead of what actually fulfils you, it will never feel satisfying—no matter how much you achieve.

167

When I finally did this exercise, I realised something surprising: The version of success I had been chasing wasn't even mine. It was a leftover definition from a career path I was no longer on. I had spent so much time running toward something that I had never stopped to ask myself if I even wanted it anymore.

And when I finally let go of that outdated version of success? I could breathe again. Clarity isn't about figuring everything out at once. It's about choosing a direction that actually fits. And the moment you do that? The exhaustion fades. The uncertainty quiets. The pressure lifts. Because now, for the first time, you're actually moving forward—not just running in circles.

So, the question is:

Are you chasing success? Or are you designing it?

Stage 2: Commitment – The Moment You Go All In

There's a moment in every major decision where hesitation creeps in, wrapping itself around your thoughts like a slow-moving fog. It doesn't feel like fear at first. It feels like prudence. Like caution. Like "just making sure." You tell yourself you need more time, more information, more signs from the universe that this is the right move. You convince yourself that waiting is strategic, that keeping one foot in the familiar is wise. But deep down, you know the truth.

You're stalling.

Not because you don't want it, but because commitment feels final. It feels irreversible. And that's terrifying.

I know this feeling well. I've lived it. For months, I hovered at the edge of a major shift in my career, a move that could redefine everything for me. I had the skills. I had the plan. But still, I hesitated. I told myself I needed more certainty before I could fully commit. I wanted a guarantee that if I leaped, I wouldn't fall. But certainty doesn't come before commitment.

It comes *from* commitment. That was my first lesson in going all in.

People think that making a big decision is the hard part. It's not. The real exhaustion comes from *not* making it. Hesitation is draining. Indecision is like carrying extra weight on your back—every day, every step, it slows you down, saps your energy, and makes everything feel heavier than it should.

I spent months in that state, one foot in my old world, one foot in my potential future. It was like standing in an open doorway, refusing to move forward but unable to step back inside. And then, one day, I asked myself a question that changed everything.

"If I'm still here in six months, hesitating, how will I feel?"

That single thought hit me harder than any fear I had about taking the leap. Because I already knew the answer. I would feel stuck. I would feel like I had wasted time. I would feel like I had let myself down, not because I had tried and failed—but because I had never truly *tried* at all. That's when I realised something crucial: Staying in indecision wasn't protecting me. It was *costing* me.

It's easy to assume that people don't commit because they're lazy or unmotivated. That's rarely the case. The real reason? Fear of failure. It's not failure itself that scares us. It's what failure *means*. If we never commit fully, we always have an excuse. "Well, I never really tried." "I wasn't all in." "I could have succeeded if I had put in more effort."

But full commitment removes that safety net. If you go all in and fail, there's nowhere to hide. And that level of exposure—of being seen trying *your absolute hardest* and still not succeeding—is what terrifies most people.

So, they hover.

They stay in the "half-in, half-out" mindset, convincing themselves they'll commit *as soon as* they feel ready. But readiness never comes. Because readiness isn't the *prerequisite* to commitment. Commitment is the *prerequisite* to readiness. You don't feel ready and then commit. You commit—and then, suddenly, you're ready.

Even when people *do* make an initial commitment, many snap back to their old ways. They get excited about a new direction, take the first few steps and then, almost like muscle memory, revert to familiar habits.

This is called the *Rubber Band Effect*—the subconscious pull back to the comfort zone.

Why does this happen? Because commitment isn't just about action. It's about identity.

If you don't *see* yourself as the kind of person who succeeds in this new path, you will always snap back to the version of yourself that feels familiar—even if that version is keeping you stuck. That's why true commitment isn't about willpower.

It's about identity shift. You don't just commit to the action. You commit to *becoming the kind of person* who follows through.

I remember the exact moment I stopped negotiating with fear. I had been hesitating on a major decision—one that required me to fully commit. For weeks, I had gone back and forth, analysing, planning, running through every possible outcome. And then, I stopped. I grabbed a notebook and wrote down one sentence that changed my entire mindset:

"I'm making this work. No more backup plans."

The moment I wrote that down, I felt something shift.

I had spent so much time thinking about *what if it doesn't work?* that I had never allowed myself to fully step into *what if it does?*

And once I committed, everything became *easier*. Not because the challenges disappeared. But because I wasn't wasting energy on doubt anymore. I had made the decision and now all that was left was execution.

If you want to stop hovering in indecision, stop snapping back to old habits and stop waiting for the *perfect* moment to commit—use this framework.

Write it down. Physically. No typing. No mental agreements. Pen to paper.

1. What are you committing to? (Make it specific and measurable.)

What is the decision you are making? Not "I want to be successful." Be precise. What are you committing to doing?

2. Why does it matter? (It has to be deeper than external validation.)

This is your emotional anchor. What is at stake if you *don't* commit? Who do you become if you *do*?

3. What is your "no-excuses" rule?

What is the one non-negotiable standard you will hold yourself to, even on the hard days?

When you write this down, something shifts. It stops being a *hope* and becomes a *decision*. And once you commit—fully, without hesitation—momentum takes care of the rest. The only thing left to do?

Go all in.

Stage 3: Execution – Turning Ideas into Action

There is always a moment, just before we take action, when the mind resists. It doesn't yell or panic—it whispers. It tells us that we need more time, that the conditions aren't quite right, that success will come more easily if we just wait a little longer. It's a quiet, insidious lie and for years, I believed it. I thought that the difference between those who succeed and those who fail came down to preparation. The ones who made it had planned better, anticipated problems in advance and ensured they had everything in place before taking the leap. So, when I found myself at a crossroads, facing a new direction I had never taken before, I did what I had always done—I strategised. I researched every possible scenario, created meticulous plans, refined my approach, and told myself that once everything was in perfect order, I would finally begin.

But that moment never came. There was always one more thing to refine, one more contingency to consider, one more reason why the timing wasn't quite right. The longer I delayed, the more I convinced myself that I simply wasn't ready yet. I was waiting for some elusive signal, some magical sense of certainty that would erase my doubts and tell me it was safe to move forward. I learned that certainty doesn't come before action. It comes because of it. Execution is not about feeling ready. It's about stepping forward *before* you feel ready.

For months, I remained stuck in this cycle, believing that I was simply being responsible. That I was ensuring success by thinking through every detail. But in reality, I wasn't preparing. I was procrastinating. Because preparation, when stretched too far, becomes avoidance in disguise. I had convinced myself that I was working toward something when, in truth, I was just avoiding failure. And the irony? Avoidance guarantees failure. Because success isn't built in theory. It is built in action.

The moment I finally took the first step, everything changed. And that first step? It was a disaster. It was clumsy, awkward, and riddled with mistakes. Nothing about it looked like success. But for the first time in months, I felt something shift. It wasn't clarity—it was momentum. The thing about action, even messy action, is that it forces the world to respond. Suddenly, I wasn't just thinking about my next move—I was making decisions in real time, adjusting based on real feedback, and seeing possibilities I couldn't have planned for. The path forward wasn't something I could have mapped out in advance. It only became visible once I started walking it.

This is why execution is the great separator. It's not about intelligence, talent, or even resources. It's about who *actually moves* when the moment comes. And the truth is, most people don't. They stay stuck in preparation, convincing themselves that once they have all the answers, they will act. But what they fail to realise is that answers don't come before action. They come because of it.

"Done is better than perfect." — Sheryl Sandberg

There is a reason so many people hesitate to take the first step, and it has nothing to do with preparation. It has to do with fear. Because action means exposure. It means putting yourself in a position where you might fail. Where others might see you struggle. Where you will have to confront the possibility that what you imagined in your head might not play out perfectly in reality. And that is terrifying.

Stage 4: Resilience – Handling Setbacks Without Losing Momentum

Most people don't fear failure itself. They fear looking like a beginner. They fear stepping into the unknown and realising that they are not immediately great at something. But the only way to get good at anything is to be terrible at it first. The only way to build confidence is by taking action when you *don't* feel confident. The only way to refine your approach is by making mistakes, learning from them, and adjusting. No one avoids the beginner stage. The only question is whether you are willing to endure it long enough to reach the expert stage.

And yet, despite knowing all this, there was a moment when I almost quit. I had taken action. I had committed fully. I had stepped into this new path with uncertainty but determination. And then, I hit a setback. The kind that makes you stop in your tracks. The kind that shakes your confidence to its core. The kind that makes you wonder if you've just made the biggest mistake of your life.

I remember sitting there, replaying the failure in my head. I had put in so much effort, invested so much time, and now it felt like it had all been for nothing. The doubt crept in. Maybe this wasn't working. Maybe I wasn't meant for this. Maybe I should cut my losses before I wasted even more time. Because that's what setbacks do. They make you feel like all your progress was an illusion. They whisper that you were never good enough to begin with.

But then a single thought—one that I didn't expect—came to me: *Life will test you, but remember—when you walk up a mountain, your legs get stronger.*

I read that line and felt it land somewhere deep inside me. Because I realised that this wasn't failure. This was the incline. I had spent so much time thinking that setbacks were a sign I was going the wrong way. But what if they meant I was exactly where I needed to be?

It was then that I understood that resilience isn't built in comfort. It is built in the moments when quitting feels like the easiest option. The struggle wasn't proof that I had failed. It was proof that I was growing.

And that's when I made the decision. I wasn't stopping. I wasn't going to let a setback define me. I wasn't going to let temporary obstacles make me forget why I started in the first place. Because this wasn't failure. **This was training.**

Most people assume that progress is a straight, upward line. That if you're meant to do something, it should feel smooth, aligned, and effortless. But that's not how it works. The hardest moments are where you gain the most strength. The failures are where you learn what truly works. The setbacks are what separate those who stop from those who succeed. The question isn't whether you'll face resistance. The question is—*what will you do when you do?*

Because the moment you push through, you realise something incredible—you were never breaking. **You were building.**

I wish I could tell you that after that moment, everything became easy. It didn't. There were still challenges. Still doubts. Still obstacles that made me question myself. But something had changed. I no longer saw setbacks as reasons to quit. I saw them as proof that I was on the right path. Every difficult moment wasn't pushing me backward—it was pushing me forward.

178

And that is what resilience really is. It's not about avoiding challenges. It's about using them to become unstoppable.

So let me ask you:

Have you ever faced a setback and convinced yourself it meant you were failing?

Have you ever wanted to quit because progress felt slower than you expected?

Have you ever mistaken challenges for signs that you were on the wrong path—when really, they were just part of the climb?

Life will test you, but remember—when you walk up a mountain, your legs get stronger.

Every time you keep going when it would be easier to quit, you are building something that cannot be broken.

And one day, you will look back at the struggles that once made you want to quit, and you will realise, they didn't stop you.

They made you.

Stage 5: Integration – Turning Success into a Repeatable Process

For a long time, success felt like something I had to chase. It was a moving target, always slightly out of reach, always requiring another sprint to keep up. I had been conditioned to believe that effort was everything, that as long as I kept pushing, the rewards would come. And they did—at first. I achieved. I climbed. I moved forward. But I also felt like I was constantly starting over, like every win was followed by the pressure to do it all again, only bigger this time.

It took me years to realise that I was playing a game designed to exhaust me. I wasn't failing, but I was operating on a model of success that wasn't built for longevity. It was built for survival. I was treating success as something I had to earn over and over, rather than something I could systematise. I was relying on effort alone, without realising that effort without structure is like trying to fill a bucket with a hole in the bottom. No matter how much you pour in, it never stays full.

The difference between those who succeed once and those who succeed consistently isn't intelligence, talent, or luck. It's design. Some people win big, but burn out, forever trying to recreate the conditions that led to their first victory. Others create a structure that makes success inevitable, predictable, repeatable. And the moment I understood that, everything changed.

I stopped thinking in terms of single achievements and started thinking in terms of systems. If I had a great month, I didn't just celebrate—I studied what worked. If I hit a goal, I didn't move blindly to the next one—I looked for patterns I could replicate. I asked myself a new set of questions:

- *What led to this success?*
- *What parts of it were random and what parts were within my control?*
- *How can I make this process work for me every time, instead of just hoping for another win?*

I wasn't chasing wins anymore. I was building a structure that made winning inevitable.

Most people assume that success comes from pushing harder, doing more, outworking everyone else. And while effort is important, it's not enough on its own. If effort were the key, the hardest-working people in the world would also be the most successful and we know that's not true. The real key is turning effort into a process that works consistently.

Think of it this way: Imagine two people trying to fill a swimming pool. One person is using a bucket, running back and forth to the water source, working as fast as they can. The other person takes the time to install a proper pipe system. The first person gets some water into the pool, but they're constantly exhausted. The second person? They might take longer to get started, but once the system is in place, the pool fills itself.

For years, I was the bucket person. I worked harder, ran faster, tried to stay ahead. But I never felt like I was catching up. And then I realised—I needed to stop chasing and start designing. I needed to build something sustainable.

So, I shifted. I stopped thinking about *effort* and started thinking about *systems*. I studied my own patterns. I found ways to automate my progress, to remove randomness from my results. Instead of hoping things would work out, I created processes that made success predictable.

And suddenly, success wasn't exhausting anymore. It was natural. It was built into my days.

Most people work toward one big goal at a time—the promotion, the deal, the milestone moment. And when they get there, they feel accomplished. But then what? They realise they have to start over. They have to do it all again, from scratch. And that's why success often feels exhausting—because it's not being treated as a process, but as a series of isolated victories.

182

But what if you stopped focusing on single wins and started focusing on a system that creates wins repeatedly? What if, instead of asking, "How can I achieve this goal?" you asked, "How can I make achieving goals automatic?"

That's the difference between effort-based success and system-based success.

When I made this shift, I started seeing results with less stress, less burnout, and less frustration. I wasn't constantly in a state of high effort. Instead, I had created a framework where small, consistent actions built up over time—creating wins not just once, but over and over.

And the best part? I no longer felt like I had to prove myself every time. My success wasn't dependent on whether I had the energy to sprint that day. It was built into the way I worked, thought, and structured my time.

If you want to turn your success into a repeatable process, here's where you start. After every win, pause and reflect. Ask yourself:

1. **What worked?** What specific actions led to your success? What were the repeatable habits, decisions, or strategies?
2. **What didn't?** What parts of the process were inefficient, draining, or unnecessary? What can you cut?

THE CEILING THAT WASN'T A CEILING

3. **What's the new system?** How can you take what worked and make it automatic, so that success happens naturally instead of requiring constant effort?

By answering these questions consistently, you start to create a blueprint for winning—one that doesn't rely on luck, motivation, or perfect circumstances.

The Architecture of Success

Looking back, I can see how every stage of this journey fit together. At the time, each stage felt disconnected, like I was simply fighting to get through the next challenge. But now, I understand the pattern.

Clarity gave me direction. It showed me where I was going, instead of just running.

Commitment forced me past hesitation. It made me stop waiting for certainty and start taking ownership of my path.

Execution created momentum. It turned ideas into action, even when I didn't feel ready.

Resilience strengthened me. It made setbacks part of the process instead of roadblocks.

Integration made success repeatable. It turned effort into structure, randomness into reliability.

Every stage built upon the one before it. Every challenge prepared me for the next. And now, I see it for what it really was—not a series of disconnected struggles, but a blueprint for how progress actually works.

If I had waited for success to come to me, I'd still be standing where I started. If I had relied on effort alone, I'd still be exhausted, running faster just to stay in place. But when I recognised the stages, when I stopped chasing and started designing—that's when everything changed.

And now, you have that same blueprint.

I'm going to ask you:

- Are you stuck, waiting for something to change?
- Are you struggling with clarity, unsure what success actually means for you?
- Are you hesitating, fearing what might go wrong instead of what could go right?
- Are you delaying action, waiting for the perfect moment?
- Are you facing setbacks, wondering if they mean you should stop?
- Or are you finally ready to integrate everything and create a success system that sustains itself?

185

Because now, you don't have to guess. You don't have to wonder if you're doing enough, if you're in the right place, if success is just about luck or timing or something that happens to other people.

Success is a design. A structure. A process.

And now?

It's yours to build.

And if there's still a voice inside you whispering, "But what if I fail?"

Remember this:

What if you fly?

Because standing at the edge of possibility is terrifying.

But soaring is only possible when you take the leap.

And the only thing left to do now is move forward.

CHAPTER 7

WHAT IF I FAIL?

—◦◇◦—

Failure doesn't announce itself with a crash. More often, it's quiet—insidious. It doesn't feel like a fall; it feels like erosion. A slow wearing down of resolve. A gradual fading of intention. A decision that at first seems inconsequential but, upon closer inspection, reveals itself as something far heavier.

Most people think failure is loud. They picture a business imploding, a career-ending mistake, a spectacular, irreversible collapse. But real failure? It sneaks up on you. It whispers in your ear that there's no harm in waiting, no shame in stepping back *just for now*, no urgency to push forward when the resistance feels too strong. It convinces you that leaving something unfinished isn't failure—it's just a choice.

And that's exactly how I failed. Not in a boardroom. Not in some high-stakes, life-defining moment. But in the most mundane and unremarkable way possible.

I had just returned from our summer holiday, feeling re-freshed and full of positivity. That kind of new-season motivation where you tell yourself, *this is it, this is when everything changes.* I was ready to commit, to finally pri-oritise my health and fitness, to become the version of myself I had always imagined.

I signed up for a sleek, high-end gym—mirrored walls, gleaming equipment, everything designed for peak per-formance. As I walked through on my induction tour, I could already see myself there, part of this world.

At first, I felt certain I was doing all the right things.

I bought expensive gym clothes—the kind that made me look like I belonged there. I researched meal plans and class timetables, overestimating how often I'd actually go. In my head, I imagined myself waking up energised, effortlessly fitting workouts into my schedule, walking out of each session stronger, fitter, more disciplined. But reality didn't match the vision.

The class times were never quite right—too early, too late, too inconvenient. And when I did make it, I spent more time watching the clock than focusing on the workout. The studios were blasted with freezing air con-ditioning, making me shiver when I should have been warming up. The air was thick with the stale scent of sweat clinging to every surface.

And the changing rooms? One look was enough. Damp floors. The rush of people. That uncomfortable silence of strangers avoiding eye contact while getting dressed. The communal showers with rogue hairs in the drains. I told myself I'd rather shower at home, where it was cleaner, where I didn't have to navigate around dripping towels and discarded shampoo bottles.

Everything felt exaggerated in my head. Every small inconvenience magnified until it became another reason not to go. At first, I told myself these were just teething problems. I needed to push through the discomfort, find my rhythm, make it part of my routine. But as the weeks passed, the anticipation of going to the gym felt heavier than the workout itself. And that's when the realisation hit me. Buying into something is not the same as doing it.

At first, I went to the gym. I showed up. I did the workouts. I walked out feeling accomplished, my muscles aching in that satisfying way that whispered, *this is working*. I imagined the results taking shape—the stronger, fitter, more disciplined version of myself that was just a few weeks away.

But excitement can be fragile. It starts with a spark, but if the fire isn't fed, it dims. And that's what happened. Little by little, the light began to fade. It wasn't dramatic or sudden—it was the slow, quiet erosion of hope. I found myself going through the motions, my heart no longer in it, wondering where my passion had gone.

It started small—skipping a session here and there because I had a packed schedule, or because I felt exhausted, or because *I just wasn't feeling it today.*

Then, the reasons became bigger.

The journey to the gym felt longer than it actually was—a trek that wasn't worth it, especially on cold, rainy evenings. The classes felt too full, the air thick with the weight of too many bodies crammed into one space. Even when I made it to a class, my mind wasn't there. I found myself glancing at the clock, counting down the minutes, waiting for the session to be over before it had even really begun. And before I knew it, I had stopped going altogether.

But I didn't tell myself I had quit. Instead, I rewrote the story.

"The gym just isn't for me, I told myself. *I prefer outdoor workouts. I'll just exercise at home instead."*

I didn't feel like I was giving up. I felt like I was making a decision. A logical, reasonable choice. One that put me in control. Until eighteen months later, when I called to cancel my membership. The receptionist checked my records. There was a pause, then a polite but unmistakable laugh.

"Oh... you've only been five times since joining."

Five.

In eighteen months.

That wasn't just inconsistency. That wasn't just losing motivation. That was total abandonment. And the worst part? I had spent so much energy convincing myself that it wasn't failure. That I hadn't given up. That I had never actually committed in the first place.

Failure isn't always a single event. More often, it's a slow process—a gradual slide through three stages that feel harmless at first.

At first, I avoided the truth. I told myself:

"I'll go next week."

"I just need to find a better time slot."

Avoidance keeps the illusion alive—the illusion that we are still committed, still making progress, still *just one decision away* from getting back on track.

It's why people leave unread emails in their inbox. It's why they let unread books sit on their shelves. It's why they hold onto gym memberships for months even though they never step foot inside.

As long as we don't acknowledge failure, we can pretend it hasn't happened yet. When I could no longer ignore it, I rationalised it away.

"The gym just isn't for me."

Rationalisation is one of the mind's strongest defence mechanisms. We take a lack of effort and disguise it as a shift in priorities.

"I'm just not a gym person."

"This doesn't align with my lifestyle."

"I'd rather invest my time elsewhere."

And for a while, I believed it. Until the receptionist's voice forced me to confront the truth.

This is the final and most dangerous stage. If we avoid it long enough and rationalise hard enough, we stop seeing our failures as moments and start seeing them as defining traits.

It stops being:

"I didn't stick to the gym."

And becomes:

"I'm just not someone who sticks with things."

We start believing we are fundamentally incapable of change. That we are just "the kind of person" who gives up, who fails, who doesn't finish what they start. And that's what makes failure so dangerous. Not the event itself—but the identity shift it creates.

Sitting there, holding my phone, I had two choices:

1. **Laugh it off.** Pretend it didn't matter. Move on.
2. **Look at it for what it was.** A reflection—not just of my gym habits, but of **how I dealt with challenges in every part of my life**.

Because failure isn't about what happened. It's about how we respond to it. This wasn't about the gym. It was about every unread book, every unfinished project, every abandoned goal. And if this was the real pattern—if failure was creeping into my life *not with explosions but with quiet unnoticed retreats*—then I had to consider:

Where else was I giving up before I ever really started?

The Three Types Of Failure: Failure Isn't The Enemy – Misunderstanding It Is

Failure has a bad reputation. It's cast as the villain in every story of success, the obstacle to be avoided at all costs. But failure isn't the problem. How we interpret failure is.

Not all failures are created equal. Some are useless, the kind of collapses that happen because of negligence, poor preparation, or a refusal to learn. Others, however, are necessary. They teach us what works by eliminating what doesn't. They act as mile markers on the road to mastery. The key is knowing the difference.

There are three types of failure, and if you can learn to categorize them properly, you can stop wasting time on failures that hold you back and start leveraging the ones that move you forward.

1. Preventable Failure: The Unforced Error

Some failures shouldn't have happened. They aren't the result of risk-taking or innovation gone wrong. They are self-inflicted wounds, the consequences of ignoring obvious warning signs, cutting corners, or assuming that effort alone is enough.

Take Blockbuster, for example. In the early 2000s, Netflix approached them with an offer to sell their company. At the time, Netflix was a struggling DVD rental-by-mail service, while Blockbuster dominated the home entertainment market. Confident in their empire, Blockbuster executives laughed at the idea. They dismissed Netflix as a niche service, assuming DVD rentals would last forever.

We all know how that story ended.

This is the tragedy of preventable failure—the failures that happen not because of forces beyond our control, but because of our own refusal to adapt. It's when we have every reason to change course, but we don't.

And that's exactly what I did with the gym.

I told myself that buying the membership was enough. That having the gear and the workout plan meant I was committed. But commitment isn't about what you buy—it's about what you do, repeatedly, over time. When I stopped showing up, I didn't immediately acknowledge it as failure. Instead, I ignored the warning signs. The slow decline in my attendance. The growing list of excuses. The creeping acceptance that I was becoming someone who "just wasn't into the gym."

And that's the insidious nature of preventable failure—it disguises itself as a shift in preference rather than a breakdown in discipline.

2. Complex Failure: When the System Works Against You

Sometimes, failure doesn't happen because of ignorance or negligence. It happens because the environment is unpredictable.

Think about Apollo 13—a space mission that, despite years of meticulous planning, nearly ended in disaster due to unforeseen technical malfunctions. Every system

196

had been tested, every variable considered, but failure still found a way in. Yet, because NASA's engineers had a deep understanding of problem-solving under pressure, they didn't let the failure defeat them. They adapted.

This kind of failure doesn't mean you were wrong—it means you were incomplete. And looking back, that was my real failure with the gym. I wasn't lazy. I wasn't uninterested. I was unprepared.

I didn't know how to structure a fitness plan. I didn't understand that muscle soreness wasn't a sign to stop, but a natural part of adaptation. I didn't have a system for keeping myself accountable. I treated effort like it was enough, but effort without guidance is just wasted energy.

Complex failure is frustrating because it feels unfair. You put in the work, but it still doesn't work out. But there's a critical distinction: this kind of failure is valuable—if you know how to use it.

3. Intelligent Failure: The Good Kind

And then, there's the best kind of failure—the kind that moves you forward.

This is what James Dyson went through while trying to invent his famous bagless vacuum. Before he landed on the final product, he created 5,127 prototypes. That means he failed 5,127 times before he got it right. But each failure wasn't wasted—it gave him new information, refining his design, improving his approach, and bringing him closer to success.

This is intelligent failure—the failure that comes from trying something new, stepping outside comfort zones, or pushing the limits of what's possible. It's failure as progress.

And looking back, that's exactly how I should have seen my gym failure.

What if, instead of seeing it as proof that I wasn't meant for the gym, I had seen it as an experiment? What if I had changed my strategy instead of quitting? What if I had focused on small wins instead of expecting instant results? What if I had treated the discomfort as part of the process rather than a sign to stop?

The truth is, the most successful people don't avoid failure—they use it. They test, refine, and iterate. They don't let failure become an excuse to stop.

At some point, we all fail. We make bad calls, we overestimate ourselves, we stumble into situations we aren't prepared for. But failure isn't the opposite of success.

It's part of success.

The difference between people who succeed and people who stay stuck isn't intelligence, talent, or luck. It's how they respond to failure.

Some people see failure as a reason to stop. Others see it as data.

And if you can learn to categorise failure—to separate the mistakes from the experiments, the avoidable from the inevitable, the useless from the valuable—then failure stops feeling like a personal attack and starts feeling like a tool.

Because in the end, the people who win aren't the ones who avoid failure. They are the ones who learn from it—and refuse to stop moving forward.

How To Move On Without Carrying The Weight Of Failure

"Failure is not the opposite of success, it's part of success." — Arianna Huffington

Failure doesn't just bruise the ego—it lingers, shaping how we see ourselves long after the moment has passed. It's never just about what went wrong; it's about the meaning we attach to it. The stories we tell ourselves after failure determine whether we grow from it or whether we shrink. We replay the missteps, the humiliation, the moments where we could have taken a different path. And instead of seeing those moments as information, as neutral data points that could guide our next steps, we turn them into proof—proof that we weren't good enough, that we weren't meant for this, that we should have never tried at all. But here's the thing: failure isn't the enemy. It's the raw material for success. The only real failure is misunderstanding what it's trying to teach you.

When people talk about resilience, they make it sound like an inborn trait, something you either have or you don't. But resilience is not genetic; it's practiced. It's built in the moments after failure—when you decide whether to retreat or to take another step forward. And that decision, the one you make after failure, is the one that shapes everything else. So, how do you move forward? How do you process failure without letting it define you? The answer is simple, but it requires work. You have to reframe it, extract the lessons, and then, most importantly, you have to act.

Step One - Reframing the Failure Story

Failure is a story. And most people tell failure stories in the worst possible way. They turn themselves into victims, painting the experience as something that happened *to* them rather than something they can learn *from.* They say, *I wasn't good enough. I should have never tried.*

This just proves I'm not meant for this. They replay the event over and over, solidifying their role as the person who lost, rather than the person who could rise again.

But what if failure is just perspective? What if it's not a dead end, but a rough draft? The best failures, the ones that ultimately lead to success, are the ones where people refuse to let the story end there. Take J.K. Rowling, for example. Before *Harry Potter* became a phenomenon, she was drowning in rejection letters. Any one of those rejections could have been the end of her story. But she didn't let it be. Instead of seeing rejection as a sign that she wasn't a real writer, she reframed it. *Each rejection letter,* she once said, *was proof that I was trying.* That small shift changed everything. Instead of internalising failure, she used it as evidence of persistence.

And that's the key. The way you tell your failure story determines what happens next. If you frame it as a sign to stop, you will. If you frame it as part of the process, you'll keep going. Imagine taking your biggest failure— something that still stings, something you hate thinking about—and rewriting it as if it were someone else's inspiring comeback story. What would change? How would the story sound if you were telling it from a place of resilience rather than regret?

The moment you take control of the narrative, failure stops feeling like an indictment. It becomes a lesson. It becomes fuel.

Step Two - Extracting the Lessons (The Three Wins Method)
The problem with failure is that it's overwhelming. It convinces us that *everything* went wrong, leaving us with no clear next steps. But failure is rarely total. Even in the moments that feel like absolute collapse, there are things that worked, however small. The trick is learning to find them.

This is why high performers don't just reflect on failure in broad terms. They break it down. They look at it piece by piece, separating the disaster from the data. And the best way to do that is to ask three simple questions:

What part of this failure was within my control? What did I learn that I wouldn't have otherwise? And what small thing actually worked, even if the whole thing didn't?

These questions shift the focus from defeat to discovery. They force you to dissect the experience, to pick apart what happened so that you can carry something forward instead of just carrying regret. Because even in the worst failures, there are things that went *right*. Maybe you lost the job, but the interview process taught you how to present yourself better. Maybe your business idea flopped, but along the way, you realised you were incredible at marketing. Maybe you embarrassed yourself in that meeting, but now, you will never show up unprepared again.

Failure is a map. If you don't analyse it, you're walking blindly into the next attempt, making the same mistakes in different ways. But when you slow down and extract the wins—the things that worked, the pieces that are worth keeping—you start to see failure for what it really is: a rough draft, a test run, a prototype for something better.

Step Three - Creating a Bounce-Back Strategy

Even after reframing failure and pulling out the lessons, there's still one problem left: confidence. Because failure doesn't just hurt—it leaves residue. It makes you hesitate. It convinces you that history will repeat itself. That's why most people get stuck. They analyse their failures, they learn from them, but they never act again—because they are afraid of reliving the fall.

The only way to break through that fear is action. But not the kind of action that overwhelms. If you're trying to bounce back from failure, the worst thing you can do is try to *force* yourself back into success overnight. That's just setting yourself up for another crash. Instead, you need micro-wins.

Think about the gym story. The mistake wasn't failing to go consistently. The mistake was assuming that commitment meant intensity, that success was about doing everything at once rather than building small habits that could be sustained. The real way to bounce back from failure isn't to overhaul your life in one massive push. It's to start with something so small, so manageable, that you can't fail. If going to the gym was too much, start with five minutes of movement at home. If writing a book felt impossible, start with a single sentence. If rebuilding confidence after failure feels like too much, start with one small action that reminds you of your competence.

This works because of the *Confidence-Competence Loop*—a simple but powerful concept in psychology that explains how small successes create momentum. When you do something small and succeed, it makes you more confident. That confidence makes you more likely to take another step. That next step builds more competence. And the cycle continues. This is how people recover from failure.

The Mercy In Second Chances

"Strange is our relationship with Allah, the Majestic. We wrong as if He sees nothing, and He forgives as if He saw nothing." – Unknown

204

Failure carries a peculiar weight because of what it convinces us about ourselves. It is not the mistake itself that lingers, but the shame, the regret, the quiet certainty that we are now marked, somehow diminished by the experience. We walk through life with our failures etched into our memories like scars, running our fingers over them again and again as if to remind ourselves not to make the same mistake twice. But there is a strange mercy in failure—one that we often overlook. Because failure, for all its weight, is not final. It does not close the door on who we are allowed to become. And yet, we often choose to believe otherwise.

This is the paradox of second chances. They exist all around us—offered by time, by opportunity, by life itself—yet we struggle to take them. Because we don't believe we are worthy of them. We believe failure has disqualified us, that if we couldn't get it right the first time, we have no business trying again. The mere existence of second chances is proof that failure does not define you. If it did, second chances would not exist.

There is a quote that has always stayed with me, one that captures the absurd beauty of human nature and the vastness of divine mercy. *"Strange is our relationship with Allah, the Majestic. We wrong as if He sees nothing, and He forgives as if He saw nothing."*

That line unearths something incredibly deep about the way we experience failure. We make mistakes—not in secret, not hidden from the world, but in full view. We falter while people watch. We stumble, sometimes spectacularly, with an audience. We convince ourselves that every flaw, every misstep, every humiliation is permanently stamped onto our identity. We assume that if someone has seen us fail, they will never look at us the same way again. And yet, life does not work that way.

The reality is that failure is never invisible. It is seen. It is witnessed. It is recorded in memories, both ours and those of the people around us. But despite this, we are still given new chances, new days, new ways forward. Just as divine mercy does not erase our wrongs but offers us a path beyond them, life itself does the same. Not because failure is ignored. Not because it is forgotten. But because it was never meant to be the end of the story.

The irony of failure is that we believe it brands us, defines us, locks us into place. But in reality, it does the opposite. It reshapes us. It forces us to learn, to grow, to adapt. It does not mark the end of our credibility—it refines it.

For all the ways that life offers second chances, we remain our own harshest judges. We hold onto our past mistakes as if they are evidence against us in a trial that never ends. We punish ourselves for things long after the world has moved on, as if self-inflicted suffering will somehow make up for what went wrong. We replay our worst moments on a loop, turning them over in our minds like a stone worn smooth from too much handling.

But why?

Why do we find it so much harder to forgive ourselves than to forgive others?

Perhaps it is because failure is intimate. We do not just remember the event—we remember the exact moment when we realized we had failed. The sinking feeling in our stomach. The heat rising in our face. The shame settling in our bones. No one else can feel those things as acutely as we can. No one else can inhabit the space inside our heads, the one where we keep records of all our wrong turns. And so, while others may forget, while they may move on, we do not.

But here is what we fail to realize: the weight of failure is not something that is *put* on us. It is something we *choose* to carry.

We assume that if failure still haunts us, it must mean we have not paid the price yet. But the only reason failure still weighs on us is because we refuse to put it down. The only reason we still feel unworthy is because we have not allowed ourselves to believe in our own redemption. The only thing stopping us from stepping forward is the belief that we do not deserve to.

But second chances are not given because we *deserve* them.

They are given because we *need* them.

The Unfinished Story

We tell ourselves that if something was meant for us, it wouldn't have been so difficult. That if a dream was truly ours, the path would have been smoother. That if we failed at something, it was life's way of saying, *this is not for you.* But that's not how life works. The gym story wasn't about fitness. It was about every moment I abandoned something—not because I lacked ability, but because I wasn't ready to endure the discomfort of real growth. I convinced myself that failure meant something wasn't meant for me, when in reality, I simply wasn't willing to struggle for it.

And how many times have we all done the same?

How many dreams have we discarded because the journey wasn't effortless? How many relationships have we let slip away—not because they couldn't work, but because they required more effort than we expected? How many opportunities have we ignored, not because they weren't valuable, but because they didn't hand us instant rewards? We mistake difficulty for a sign that something isn't meant for us, when in reality, it's often the very opposite. The things most worth having rarely come easily.

We walk away because growth is uncomfortable. Because change requires more than just desire—it demands endurance. Because the fear of failing again weighs heavier than the possibility of succeeding eventually. And so, we convince ourselves that the door is locked, when really, we just stopped knocking.

Failure convinces us that the story has ended. That the opportunity has passed. That whatever chance we had, we lost. But the truth? The door was never locked—we just chose to stop reaching for the handle.

Life does not demand perfection. It does not require that we get everything right the first time. It does not close doors permanently just because we stumbled at the threshold. Life, like divine mercy, does not measure worth by the absence of mistakes. It measures it by the willingness to try again.

We assume second chances are rare, but they are everywhere, waiting for us to stop running from our own potential.

Failure is not a punishment. It is an invitation.

An invitation to stand back up. To see what's possible beyond the moment of defeat. To recognise that the only real failure is the refusal to try again.

What if the only thing standing between you and success isn't your ability, but your willingness to get back up? What if the dreams you've convinced yourself weren't meant for you were simply waiting for you to push through the discomfort? What if the only difference between those who succeed and those who don't isn't talent or luck—but the ability to keep going when every part of them wants to quit?

Because failure doesn't mean you weren't meant for something.

It simply asks:

Will you try again?

"It's not whether you get knocked down, it's whether you get up." — Vince Lombardi

CHAPTER 8

LEADERSHIP UNCHAINED: INFLUENCE WITHOUT AUTHORITY

---◦◇◦---

The table was a long stretch of polished mahogany, set with gleaming glassware and delicate silverware that caught the flickering glow of candlelight. The room hummed with the low murmur of voices—some confident, some cautious, all orbiting around the same gravitational pull: influence. It was a battlefield of ideas disguised as polite conversation rather than just a simple dinner. The air carried the scent of slow-roasted lamb and freshly baked bread, but beneath it lingered the quiet competition for control.

At one end of the table, a senior executive commanded the room without effort. His voice had that practiced cadence of someone used to being heard—steady, unwavering, self-assured. He spoke of market trends, technological shifts, and the inevitable restructuring of the industry over the next five years. He wasn't asking for opinions. He was declaring the future.

Around him, the others nodded in unspoken agreement, not necessarily because they agreed, but because they knew how these conversations worked. A dinner like this had an invisible hierarchy. Some voices shaped the discussion, while others simply absorbed it. There was no malice in it—just the natural order of power in motion.

And then I noticed her.

Seated two places down, a woman rested her hands lightly on the linen-covered table. She wasn't checked out. She wasn't detached. If anything, she was more engaged than anyone else. Her eyes tracked every exchange, her head tilting slightly at moments of contradiction, a subtle shift in posture when someone glossed over a crucial point. Twice, she opened her mouth to interject, only to stop as another voice filled the gap.

Her face didn't change, but I saw it—the flicker of hesitation, the battle between patience and the urge to speak. The quiet frustration of a thought forming with nowhere to land. She was waiting. Calculating. Deciding whether to push through or let the moment pass.

I knew that feeling.

The conversation looped in predictable patterns, reinforcing its own conclusions. Not because anyone was wrong, but because the same few voices dictated the rhythm. It was a closed circuit. And then, a pause. Not silence—just a momentary dip in energy, the kind that happens when one thread is exhausted but the next hasn't begun.

She spoke.

"I was just thinking," she said, her voice measured but unwavering, "we're so focused on the risks of this change that we haven't really considered the opportunity cost of not acting. What happens if we do nothing?"

Something changed. Heads turned. Eyes refocused. One of the executives, mid-sip, lowered his glass slightly. Another leaned back, reconsidering.

She hadn't spoken loudly. She hadn't interrupted. But she had done something far more powerful.

She had reframed the conversation.

Instead of letting the discussion roll past her, she had anchored it to a question that couldn't be ignored. It wasn't about forcing her way in. It was about making the room want to follow where she was going.

Someone finally responded. "That's a good point. What does that look like in numbers?"

And suddenly, the conversation expanded.

The conversation evolved from focusing solely on risk to exploring missed opportunities, long-term strategy, and the unintended consequences of playing it safe. She had been sitting there the entire time with the same insights, the same expertise. She didn't need to dominate the room—she just needed an opening.

That moment stayed with me. It made me realise how often discussions, decisions, even entire strategies are shaped not by the best ideas, but by the voices that find the space to be heard.

Leadership isn't about volume. It isn't about title or authority. It's about knowing when to create the space for momentum to shift.

And sometimes, that's all influence is—not forcing change, but allowing it.

Lao Tzu once wrote, *"A leader is best when people barely know they exist, when their work is done, their aim fulfilled, they will say: we did it ourselves."*

That moment at the dinner table taught me that real leadership isn't given—it's created. And the secret to creating it is influence, not authority.

The Three Pillars of Influence-Based Leadership

Leadership is not given—it is created. And what creates it? Not titles, not power, not the ability to command a room with sheer presence. Influence. The most effective leaders—the ones people follow willingly, not because they have to, but because they want to—master three things: trust, clarity, and momentum. These aren't abstract qualities; they are the architecture of influence, the reason some people can walk into a room and shift the entire energy without raising their voice.

We've all seen it happen. A person without an official title quietly commands respect, their voice carrying weight in conversations where they technically hold no power. Others, burdened with authority on paper, struggle to get anyone to listen. Influence is not a gift of circumstance; it is the result of mastering these three principles.

Trust - The Foundation of Influence

Trust is the currency of leadership. If people don't trust you, nothing else matters. They won't follow you, they won't believe you, and they won't buy into your vision. Titles don't build trust. Authority doesn't build trust. Repeated, consistent proof of character does.

Think about the people you trust most in your life. It's not their job title that makes them trustworthy—it's their reliability, their consistency, the simple fact that when they say something, you believe it. Now, flip that to a work setting. Have you ever had a boss whose title demanded respect, but whose actions never earned it? Someone who spoke in grand promises but never followed through?

Now, compare that to a colleague—someone without formal authority but who everyone instinctively turns to when things get difficult. Someone who, without being asked, always delivers. That's influence.

The difference between the two comes down to *The Trust Equation:*

(Credibility + Reliability + Authenticity) / Self-Interest

Credibility: Do people believe you know what you're talking about?

Reliability: Do you follow through on what you say, time and time again?

Authenticity: Are you consistent in your words and actions, or do you perform based on the audience?

Self-Interest: If people sense you're acting only for yourself, everything else collapses.

217

This formula explains why some leaders struggle despite their expertise. If self-interest outweighs credibility, reliability, and authenticity, people will see right through it. No one follows someone they feel is only looking out for themselves.

A large corporation hires an outside consultant to help with a restructuring initiative. On paper, their credentials are impressive. Experience, degrees, high-profile clients. But the moment they step into the room, they are met with silence. No engagement. No buy-in.

Why?

Because the last consultant made big promises and disappeared. The team has been burned before and now, trust is gone. They've learned that "expert" doesn't always mean dependable.

This isn't just a consultant's problem. It's a universal leadership challenge. Every time you step into a role where trust isn't automatic, you face the same reality: your authority means nothing until you prove yourself.

How did this consultant build trust from scratch?

They didn't jump in with 'expert advice'—they started by listening. They asked thoughtful questions instead of making assumptions. They followed through on small commitments before asking for bigger ones. They focused on what mattered to the team, not just what looked good on a report.

Slowly, resistance softened. The team started to listen. Not because they had to, but because they wanted to.

Take a hard look at your influence. Ask yourself:

Do I have credibility? (Do people see me as competent and knowledgeable?)

Am I reliable? (Do my actions match my words?)

Am I authentic? (Do I show up consistently as myself, or do I adapt to what I think people want?)

Do people believe I have their best interests at heart?

Trust isn't built in a day. But it can be lost in a moment.

The Trust Audit (Self-Assessment)

Trust is not built on authority—it's built on credibility, reliability, authenticity, and alignment with others' interests. Take this self-assessment to gauge where you stand.

Rate yourself from 1 (Rarely) to 5 (Always) on the following statements:

Credibility:

- I consistently demonstrate expertise in my area of work.
- People trust my judgment and seek my advice on key decisions.
- When I speak on a topic, I ensure my facts and insights are well-researched.

Reliability:

- I follow through on my commitments, even when it's inconvenient.
- People know they can depend on me in high-stakes situations.
- I communicate openly when I can't meet a deadline, rather than disappearing.

Authenticity:

- I remain consistent in my values and behaviour, regardless of the audience.
- I don't perform for approval—I lead in a way that aligns with my true self.
- My colleagues and team members feel like they know the *real* me.

Self-Interest Check:

- I make decisions that benefit the collective, not just myself.

- People see me as someone who considers their needs, not just my own goals.
- I balance ambition with genuine care for those I work with.

Scoring & Reflection

- **40-50 Points:** You have strong trust-based influence. Continue refining how you lead.
- **30-39 Points:** Trust is solid but focus on areas where you can build deeper credibility, reliability, or authenticity.
- **Below 30 Points:** Identify specific areas where trust may be lacking. What patterns do you notice? How can you improve your leadership reputation?

Clarity - The Key to Alignment

People don't resist leadership. They resist confusion. If people don't understand where they're being led, they won't follow.

Have you ever been in a meeting where someone presented a "vision" so convoluted that it left you more confused than inspired? A speech so full of jargon and buzzwords that you nodded along but internally checked out?

That's what happens when clarity is missing.

"If you can't explain it simply, you don't understand it well enough." – Albert Einstein

A CEO stands before their leadership team, unveiling a bold, multi-year strategy. They talk about "leveraging synergies," "driving scalable efficiencies" and "unlocking value streams."

The executives nod. They smile.

But behind their polite expressions? Confusion.

No one challenges the CEO. But in the days that follow:

The marketing team interprets it one way.

The operations team assumes it means something else.

The frontline managers have no clue how it impacts their day-to-day work.

Instead of alignment, there is fragmentation.

The breakthrough happens when a senior leader asks, "If we had to explain this to a new employee in one sentence, what would we say?"

Silence.

Then, the fluff is stripped away. The vision is refined. They land on one clear, compelling statement that makes sense to everyone. That's when things start moving.

The One-Sentence Vision Formula

Want to test your clarity? Use this:

"We exist to [achieve this outcome] by [doing this specific action] so that [this benefit occurs]."

If you can't say it simply, no one will follow it confidently. Clarity is the bridge between an idea and action. Without it, influence fails before it begins.

Example 1:

Unclear vision: "We want to be the best customer-centric company in the industry."

Clear vision: "We help people make smarter financial decisions by offering transparent, data-driven insights so that they feel in control of their future."

Example 2:

Unclear vision: "We're building a more inclusive workplace."

Clear vision: "We foster a culture where every voice is heard by implementing bias-free hiring and leadership development so that everyone feels valued and empowered."

Try writing your leadership vision in one sentence using the formula. Then ask:

223

- Does it make sense immediately?
- Would a new employee understand it?
- Would my team know how to act on it?

Momentum - The Engine of Progress

Momentum is a strange thing. It's both fragile and un-stoppable. It's the gust of wind that carries a ship forward, but only if the sails are raised at the right time. It's the domino effect, where one small push leads to an avalanche of movement. And yet, momentum is also one of the most misunderstood forces in leadership and success.

People assume it comes from big, strategic moves—a groundbreaking idea, a revolutionary shift, a bold leap into the unknown. But that's the lie. The truth is quieter, less glamorous. Momentum doesn't come from massive plans. It comes from one small win—one concrete action that creates visible movement.

The problem? We are wired to chase perfection before progress. We obsess over the big picture, trying to design an ideal outcome before we take the first step. We tell ourselves we need more research, more alignment, more clarity. And before we know it, the momentum we could have built is already lost.

That's why most big plans fail, but small wins succeed.

A team gathers for a high-stakes project. The vision is bold, the stakes are high, and the initial energy is electrifying. They strategise, analyse, and debate. They create slide decks filled with projections, charts, and forecasts. They map out contingencies for every possible failure.

And then, nothing happens.

The excitement fades. Meetings become routine. Deadlines quietly slip by. And soon, what was once an ambitious transformation becomes another forgotten initiative. This isn't an isolated case. It's the fate of countless projects, goals, and even personal aspirations. Grand plans lose steam when action is delayed. The longer an idea remains theoretical, the more resistance builds against it. But contrast this with teams—or individuals—who start small. They don't wait for the perfect plan. They find one small, undeniable win that proves progress is possible. And that small victory changes everything.

A leadership team was tasked with launching a major internal transformation initiative. The potential impact was enormous. But after months of planning, there was no visible progress.

Teams had lost motivation.

Meetings had become repetitive.

Progress had slowed to a crawl.

The issue wasn't with intelligence or effort, and that was clear. The issue was rooted in a lack of movement.

Then, one executive asked a deceptively simple question:

"What's the smallest thing we can execute in the next 90 days that will prove this works?"

That single shift in mindset changed everything.

Instead of trying to overhaul the entire system, the team focused on launching one small but visible win:

A pilot project that didn't require layers of approval.

A measurable success that people could see immediately.

A shift in energy that reignited engagement.

And suddenly, the energy that had been lost returned.

Within weeks, the transformation went from a stalled discussion to a visible movement. Not because the strategy was flawless, but because people needed to see progress to believe in it. This isn't just a story about leadership. It's the formula for any type of change—whether it's launching a business, creating a habit, or rebuilding after failure.

Most people assume motivation leads to action. But the reality? Action creates motivation.

We think we need to feel inspired to start. But in reality, the smallest action—getting up, moving, making a decision—creates the very motivation we were waiting for. The secret is to engineer the first win.

When you see proof that a small step leads to visible progress, your brain rewires itself. It stops focusing on the risk of failure and starts focusing on the potential for momentum.

"You don't have to see the whole staircase, just take the first step." – Martin Luther King Jr.

The 90-Day Momentum Plan

Instead of waiting for the perfect plan, ask:

What's one action we can complete in 90 days?

How will we measure its impact?

How will this create confidence for the next step?

Because when something works—even in a small way—it's much easier to build on it.

Small wins—executed consistently—create an unstoppable flywheel of momentum.

The Momentum Maintenance Plan

Momentum isn't a one-time event—it's something you must sustain. Here's how:

1. Identify Your Smallest Meaningful Win

Ask yourself:

What is one high-impact action that can be achieved in the next 30–90 days?

How can this prove progress to the team, leadership, or key stakeholders?

2. Make It Visible

Momentum is psychological; people need to see progress to believe in it.

How can you track and showcase this win publicly?

3. Build on It Immediately

Once you achieve a small win, don't pause—leverage it.

What's the next logical step that will reinforce the momentum?

4. Expect Slowdowns—And Pre-empt Them

What are the likely obstacles?

How can you counter them before they derail progress?

Because sustained momentum isn't about motivation—it's about making success feel inevitable.

Without trust, no one will follow you. Without clarity, no one will understand you. Without momentum, no one will move with you. The best leaders don't force people to act. They create the conditions where action becomes natural.

Leading Without Authority

Power, in the traditional sense, is the ability to command. It is the authority granted by position, the leverage that comes with a title, the weight of hierarchy. But true leadership—the kind that actually drives change—is about leverage.

Leverage comes from influence, regardless of job title. And influence is not about standing at the top of an organisational chart; it is about knowing how to move things from the middle, how to shift opinions, how to create momentum even when you don't have official control.

People assume that decisions happen in boardrooms, at executive meetings, or in high-stakes presentations. But most real change happens before those meetings even begin. It happens in conversations over coffee, in quiet moments of persuasion, in the subtle shaping of ideas before they ever become formal proposals. The leaders who create change don't force decisions—they build networks that make decisions happen.

The Power of Social Capital

Think about the most influential person in your workplace or industry. It is probably not the CEO. It is the person others turn to for advice, the one whose opinion carries weight in a meeting even when they are not the most senior. It is the person who, when they support an idea, makes others feel like it is already a foregone conclusion. That is social capital.

Social capital is the currency of influence. It is built over time through credibility, trust, and the ability to connect people. And in many cases, it is more powerful than formal authority. A person with high social capital can move mountains without ever issuing a command. They don't have to push through bureaucracy, because they already have allies in the right places. They don't have to justify their ideas endlessly, because their track record makes others trust their instincts. They don't have to ask for permission, because by the time leadership is aware of the idea, it already has momentum.

In a large corporation known for its rigid hierarchy, a mid-level manager sat at their desk, staring at a problem that seemed too big to solve. The company's system for handling customer complaints was outdated and ineffi-cient, leading to frustrated clients and wasted resources. The problem was obvious. The solution was even clearer. But the challenge was daunting: They had no of-ficial authority to change company policy and the estab-lished process for proposing changes was slow, bureau-cratic, and resistant to anything that deviated from the status quo.

Most employees in this position would have accepted de-feat. They would have sent an email, cc'd the right peo-ple, and waited for leadership to ignore it. They would have buried the issue under the weight of company poli-tics and moved on. But this manager understood some-thing fundamental—authority is overrated and influence is what actually moves things.

Instead of submitting a formal proposal that would likely be dismissed, they started small. Over casual conversa-tions, they brought up the issue in passing, gauging reac-tions, seeing where the resistance might be. They spoke to colleagues in different departments, gathering firsthand experiences that confirmed what they already knew: the inefficiency was costing the company far more than anyone realised. They didn't pitch the solution out-right. They simply let the problem become part of the internal conversation, allowing others to recognise the flaws for themselves.

Over time, key figures within the company—people who held no formal leadership titles but whose voices mattered—began to echo the same concerns. Executives started hearing about it through informal channels. By the time the idea was formally presented to leadership, it wasn't a radical proposal from one mid-level employee. It was an obvious, well-supported shift that seemed like the next logical step. The decision-makers believed they were responding to a necessary change, not conceding to an individual's suggestion. The policy was updated, the system improved, and the organisation moved forward—not because of a top-down decision, but because of bottom-up momentum.

That is the power of social capital. Change happens when enough people believe it is inevitable. The most effective leaders don't fight for authority. They build networks of trust, planting seeds of influence long before anyone realizes a shift is coming.

The Influence Network Map

In any workplace, influence isn't just about what you know—it's about **who** amplifies your ideas.

Step 1: Identify Key Players

Think about the people who hold influence in your environment:

Decision-Makers: Who formally makes the big calls?

Informal Influencers: Who doesn't have a high title but shapes discussions?

Connectors: Who bridges gaps between different groups?

Gatekeepers: Who controls access to opportunities?

Step 2: Map Your Current Position

- Who do you already have strong relationships with?
- Who do you need to build trust with?
- Where are the gaps in your influence network?

Step 3: Strengthen Your Network Intentionally

- **Strengthen Existing Ties** – Offer value to the relationships you already have.
- **Build New Connections** – Find shared interests before seeking favours.
- **Create Visibility** – Ensure your work reaches the right people

Sketch your influence network. Where are your strongest connections? Where do you need to invest more effort?

Framing Ideas for Maximum Buy-In

People resist being told what to do. It is one of the most predictable, deeply ingrained reactions in human nature. It is why a child will suddenly crave the very toy they had no interest in until another child reaches for it. It is why employees bristle at sudden organisational changes, even if those changes are objectively beneficial. It is why the moment something feels mandatory, we instinctively look for ways to push back. The irony is that this resistance has nothing to do with the idea itself—it has everything to do with how the idea is introduced.

People don't reject ideas because they are bad. They reject them because they feel imposed, forced, or dictated from above. The same decision, reframed differently, can go from being met with hostility to being embraced with enthusiasm. If someone feels ownership over an idea, if they see themselves reflected in it, they will fight to make it work. But if they feel like it is being done to them rather than shaped with them, even the most well-intentioned changes will feel like a burden.

In leadership, this is the difference between compliance and commitment. A compliant team will do what they are told—but only because they have to, and only as long as they are being watched. A committed team will own the outcome because they feel like they had a hand in shaping it. The difference between the two is not logic. It is framing.

At a mid-sized company facing rising inefficiencies, leadership had decided to overhaul internal processes to streamline workflows. On paper, the move was logical, inevitable even. Every data point led to the same conclusion—without this shift, the company would lose time, money, and productivity. Yet when leadership introduced the change to employees, they were met with frustration, resistance, and pushback.

Employees weren't rejecting efficiency. No one wakes up hoping to be less productive. But they were rejecting the narrative they were being given. The message they heard was, *We are cutting inefficiencies*, which felt like a euphemism for, *You've been working wrong, and we are here to fix you.* The initiative felt like a top-down directive rather than an opportunity for improvement. It felt like something being done *to* them rather than *with* them.

The manager leading the initiative recognised the flaw— not in the idea itself, but in how it was being framed. They stepped back and reframed the conversation. Instead of saying, *We need to cut inefficiencies,* they asked, *How can we free up time so you can focus on higher-impact work?* Instead of presenting a finalised plan, they invited employees to help shape it. Instead of imposing a system, they asked, *What's the best way to make this work for you?*

The response was immediate. Employees who had initially resisted the initiative began offering insights, providing solutions, and engaging with the process. They weren't just tolerating the change—they were invested in making it successful. The fundamental shift? The employees now saw it as their own.

This wasn't manipulation. It was simply understanding how people think. When people feel like they are part of the process, their mindset shifts from defensive to collaborative. Resistance softens because they no longer see the idea as something foreign imposed on them, but as something they are shaping alongside leadership.

Psychologists have long studied this phenomenon in behavioural economics and negotiation theory. One of the most well-documented principles in persuasion is the *Endowment Effect*, which states that people place higher value on things they feel ownership over. This is why we are more likely to defend an idea we came up with, even if it was identical to an idea someone else had proposed. Ownership changes perception.

Apple's legendary marketing approach has leveraged this for decades. When Steve Jobs introduced the first iPod, he didn't tell people, *You need a portable music player.* He framed it as *1,000 songs in your pocket,* instantly making it feel like something personal, something that belonged to the user. The same applies to leadership. If people see themselves in an idea, they will champion it. If they don't, they will resist it.

Every great leader, whether in business, politics, or social movements, understands that people are not moved by facts alone. They are moved by how those facts are presented. Two leaders can introduce the exact same idea, with the exact same data, and see completely different responses—one being ignored, the other gaining immediate traction. The difference isn't in the quality of the idea. It's in how the message is delivered.

Leaders who master framing don't rely on force. They don't try to overpower resistance with logic alone. They understand that the key to influence isn't making people comply—it's making them believe the idea was theirs all along.

And this concept applies to areas outside the professional field too. This concept applies to personal relationships, where connection and involvement are key in reducing defensiveness and increasing cooperation. Where making people feel values, heard, and part of the process can completely shape the outcome.

Mastering the Push-Pull Balance

Influence is an art, not a science, and like all forms of art, it requires a deep understanding of balance. Some leaders mistake influence for control, assuming that the louder they push their ideas, the more likely people are to comply. Others take the opposite approach, so afraid of pushing too hard that they default to endless accommodation, afraid to take a stance at all. Both strategies fail. Influence is not about forcing outcomes, nor is it about surrendering to the will of others—it is about knowing when to apply pressure and when to step back.

The best leaders understand this instinctively. They recognise when to assert their position with clarity and when to allow space for others to reach conclusions on their own. They know that people don't like being forced into decisions, but they also know that without direction, nothing moves forward. This is the essence of the push-pull balance: knowing when to lead with conviction and when to listen with openness.

A senior executive was in the middle of a delicate negotiation. The company he represented was looking to form a partnership with a vendor that could bring immense value—but the vendor was reluctant. The risks felt too high, the unknowns too many. The usual approach would have been to push harder: lay out the financial incentives, stress the strategic benefits, present a polished case. Instead, the executive chose a different path.

First, they pushed—but not aggressively. They clearly articulated why the partnership made sense, highlighting the upside in a way that was direct but not overbearing. Then, they pulled back, shifting the focus from persuasion to curiosity. Rather than countering every hesitation with an argument, they asked a simple but powerful question: *What are your biggest concerns?* The moment the vendor started talking, something shifted. The focus was no longer on *convincing*—it was on *understanding*.

The executive took notes, absorbed the concerns, and instead of steamrolling past them, incorporated them into the conversation. They demonstrated flexibility where it mattered, but they also remained firm on the key areas that were non-negotiable. The vendor, initially hesitant, began to lean in. Not because they had been out-argued, but because they felt heard. By the end of the conversation, the deal was signed.

This is how real influence works. Push too hard, and you create resistance. Pull too much, and you lose direction. The real skill is knowing when to do which.

People don't like being strong-armed into decisions, but they also don't like feeling lost. If you are too aggressive in trying to win people over, they will instinctively push back, even against ideas that might benefit them. If you are too passive, they will disengage, seeing you as unconvincing or uncertain.

The best leaders recognise the natural rhythm of human decision-making. They know that the moment someone senses they are being *sold* something, their defences go up. They also know that if they leave too much ambiguity, people will hesitate, waiting for someone else to make the first move.

There is a psychological dynamic at play here. Research in negotiation shows that people feel more committed to a decision when they believe they reached it themselves. This is why some of the most effective communicators don't force conclusions—they guide people toward them. Instead of saying, *Here's what you should do,* they frame the conversation in a way that makes the other party feel like they arrived at the decision organically.

Think about the last time you had to make a major decision. If someone aggressively pushed you in one direction, chances are, you hesitated—even if the choice made logical sense. But if someone created an environment where you could explore your concerns, weigh your options, and see the value for yourself, you likely felt more confident in your choice. That's the push-pull balance in action.

Leaders who rely solely on pressure often find that their influence is short-lived. People may comply in the moment, but their buy-in is superficial. The moment they feel like they've been strong-armed into something, they start looking for an escape route. This is why people resist hard sales tactics, why employees resent top-down mandates, and why leaders who try to dominate discussions often find themselves surrounded by silence rather than engagement.

In psychology, this is known as the *Backfire Effect*— when people are confronted too aggressively with an idea, they don't just reject it; they double down on their original beliefs. Instead of shifting their perspective, they become more entrenched in their opposition. The harder you push, the more they dig in. This is why the best negotiators, leaders, and influencers know when to ease off the pressure and let people come to their own conclusions.

On the other end of the spectrum, there is the danger of *too much* pulling—too much accommodation, too much deference. Leaders who are afraid to push at all risk losing their authority. They become so focused on listening and adapting that they fail to take a stand. This leads to indecision, lack of direction, and ultimately, stagnation.

When a leader constantly pulls, they create an environment where no one knows what's expected. Meetings become endless loops of discussion without resolution. Teams hesitate, unsure of which direction to move in. Momentum stalls. At some point, leadership requires decisiveness. It requires the ability to say, *Here's the path forward.* The most effective leaders address them and then make the call.

Mastering the push-pull balance requires self-awareness. It requires paying close attention to how people react, adjusting your approach in real time and knowing when to lean in and when to step back.

When you sense resistance, ask yourself: *Am I pushing too hard?* If people are nodding but not engaging, if they seem defensive or withdrawn, it may be a sign that you need to shift to listening mode. Instead of arguing harder, ask more questions. Give people space to voice their hesitations. Make them feel heard before pushing forward.

When you sense hesitation, ask yourself: *Am I pulling too much?* If people seem lost, uncertain, or stuck in endless deliberation, it may be time to assert direction. Instead of waiting for consensus that may never come, provide clarity. Lay out a vision. Set the next step in motion.

Great leaders don't force people to follow them. They create the conditions where people *want* to follow. They push when necessary, pull when needed, and most importantly, they recognise that influence isn't about control—it's about understanding when to lead and when to let others take the lead themselves.

Influence is Leadership

There was a moment early in my career when I believed that being right was all that mattered. I assumed that if you did your research, built a logical case, and presented your argument with clarity, people would naturally agree. After all, truth speaks for itself. Or at least, that's what I thought. It was a belief that had served me well in school, in structured environments where answers were either correct or incorrect. But the professional world— the world of decision-making, leadership, and influence—wasn't like that at all.

I had spent weeks on a proposal. It wasn't just a suggestion; it was a carefully built case. The problem was clear, the solution practical, and the financial projections backed by data. I had accounted for risks, pre-empted objections, and structured the entire presentation in a way that, to me, felt airtight. When the day came, I walked into the meeting room with quiet confidence, expecting my work to speak for itself. I presented my findings, laid out the logic, walked through the numbers, and concluded with a firm recommendation. Then I sat back, waiting for the response.

It was underwhelming. A few polite nods. A couple of noncommittal follow-up questions. No real engagement. The conversation moved on and just like that, my proposal faded into irrelevance. I had done everything right, but I had accomplished nothing.

A little later in the meeting, someone else made a similar request. Almost identical, in fact. The same type of investment. The same level of risk. The same general benefits. And yet, this time, the room shifted. People leaned in. They asked questions—not vague, polite ones, but real ones. There was energy in the discussion, a sense of momentum. By the time it was over, there was not just approval, but enthusiasm. It felt like a collective decision.

I sat there, trying to mask my frustration, but inside, I was asking myself: *What just happened?*

I replayed that moment in my head over and over, dissecting every detail. It wasn't hierarchy—the person who made the second request wasn't in a more senior position than me. It wasn't the data—our cases were equally strong. The difference wasn't in what was being said, but in how it was being framed.

They created a sense of urgency rather than simply presenting facts. Instead of making a case for approval, they framed it as the next logical step in a journey that was already underway. They didn't position their request as a question; they made it feel inevitable.

I realised something fundamental: *The best ideas don't always win. The best-framed ideas do.*

I had walked into that meeting trying to justify my request. They had walked in trying to inspire action. I had expected people to see the logic of my case and simply agree. They had made sure that agreeing felt like the natural thing to do.

Looking back, I can see why I struggled with this concept for so long. I had always believed that logic was enough. That work spoke for itself. That the right decision, when presented clearly, would naturally be chosen. But that's not how influence works.

The more I observed, the more I saw that influence wasn't about pushing harder. It was about making people feel like the decision was already theirs. The leaders who got the most buy-in weren't always the most senior, but they knew how to align their message with what others cared about. The teams that moved the fastest weren't necessarily the ones with the best strategy, but they had leaders who knew how to keep momentum alive. The decisions that stuck weren't always the most rational, but they were the ones that felt necessary, urgent, and aligned with an existing path forward.

Leadership wasn't about authority. It was about influence. And influence wasn't about control—it was about creating the conditions where the right decision felt like the obvious one. That was the lesson I took from that meeting and once I understood it, everything changed.

Leadership is not about waiting for permission. It's not about having the most seniority or the loudest voice. It's not about forcing decisions through sheer willpower. It's about creating trust so that people believe in you. It's about creating clarity so that people understand the path forward. And it's about generating momentum so that action feels inevitable.

I had thought influence was about being right. But I learned that it's about being heard. If leadership were only about authority, my proposal would have been approved that day. But leadership is about influence and influence is about making things happen—even when no one is required to listen to you.

So, the question is not whether you have the authority to lead. The question is: *Where will you create your influence?*

Real leaders don't wait for permission. They create influence and make things happen.

CHAPTER 9

FROM SUCCESS TO SIGNIFICANCE: CRAFTING YOUR LEGACY

——•◦◇◦•——

There are moments in life when time slows down and the world as you once understood it fractures. These moments do not announce themselves. They do not come with fanfare or warning. Instead, they arrive quietly, settling into your bones before you even realise they have rewritten the rules of your existence.

For me, that moment came when my father passed away.

I remember standing there, surrounded by people, their voices a dull hum against the backdrop of something far heavier—grief, yes, but also realisation. I had spent my life chasing achievement, believing that success was measured in tangible things. And yet, standing in that room, none of it mattered. My father's legacy was not in the things he owned. It was in the lives he had touched.

I watched as people gathered, not to speak of his career, his possessions, or the accolades he had accumulated, but to recall the way he had made them feel. The kindness he had extended when no one else had noticed. The lessons he had imparted, not through instruction, but through example. It was in their eyes that I saw what I had missed all along: true success is not about what we take from the world, but what we leave behind.

For the first time in my life, I prayed for something beyond myself. My prayers had always been for strength, for clarity, for success in the world I was building. But that night, I prayed for him. For peace. For something beyond this fleeting existence. And in doing so, I understood that legacy isn't built in the future. It is shaped in the choices we make every single day.

This realisation did not come gently. It was not a comforting epiphany. It was unsettling. Because if success was not what I had been led to believe, then what had I been working toward? What had I been sacrificing for? And if the things I once valued held no meaning in the end, what, then, did?

It is one thing to know this in theory—to hear that life is about impact, not accumulation. It is another thing entirely to feel it, to have it crack open your understanding of the world. And once you see it, you cannot unsee it.

The weight of this knowledge sat heavy on my chest. I could not go back to chasing the same goals in the same way. I had to reimagine success, not as something to be attained but as something to be given.

And so, I made a decision.

I would no longer measure my life by what I achieved, but by what I contributed. I would not seek only to succeed, but to ensure that my success carried others with it. And perhaps most importantly, I would not let my knowledge, my lessons, my hard-earned wisdom die with me.

Because the truth is, the most painful thing about understanding legacy too late is realising how much you could have done if you had known earlier.

History has a way of teaching us what we most need to learn—if we are willing to listen.

There is a story I have always found particularly powerful. It is the story of Hajar (RA), left in the barren desert with her infant son, Ismail (AS). She had no resources, no certainty, no clear path forward. But she did not allow fear to paralyse her. Instead, she moved.

She ran between the hills of Safa and Marwah, not knowing whether her efforts would lead to salvation. And only after she had exhausted every possibility, only after she had acted with full conviction despite her uncertainty, did relief come. Water sprung from the ground beneath her son's feet. The well of Zamzam—an eternal source of sustenance, one that still exists today—was born from the struggle of a woman who refused to wait for help to arrive.

Her story is the essence of *tawakkul*—true reliance on God—not in passive waiting, but in taking action while trusting deeply in divine wisdom and mercy.

"Relief often comes when we least expect it—but only after we take action." – Unknown

I think of this story often.

Because legacy, like faith, requires action before certainty. It is not about knowing the outcome in advance. It is about moving forward, even when the road is unclear.

When I made the decision to change my life, I did not have a clear map. There was no guarantee that it would work, no promise of success. I was walking into the unknown. I left behind the safety of structure, the comfort of predictability. I abandoned everything I had spent years building in favour of something I could not yet see.

And yet, something inside me knew.

Legacy is not created in the moments when things are easy. It is forged in the moments when you choose to keep going, even when the road is uncertain. When you trust that the steps you take today will lead somewhere meaningful—even if you cannot yet see where.

That was the hardest lesson to learn.

But I understood that if I did not take the risk, if I did not move forward, I would spend the rest of my life wondering what could have been. And I was not willing to carry that weight.

There is a pattern to history, though we often fail to recognise it in real-time. What feels like failure is often the first step toward something greater.

Take the Treaty of Hudaybiyyah. When the Prophet Muhammad (SAW) and his companions set out for Makkah to perform Umrah, they were stopped and forced into a treaty that seemed entirely unjust. The terms were one-sided. It felt like a loss. His followers were devastated. They had come so far, only to be turned away.

And yet, what seemed like a setback was actually a setup. Within two years, the treaty led to the peaceful conquest of Makkah—something that would not have been possible if they had forced their way in that day.

"Not every closed door is a failure. Sometimes, what feels like a step backward is actually a step toward something greater." – Unknown

How often in life do we fight for doors to open, only to later realise that their closing was the very thing that made success possible?

I have had moments like that. Moments when deals fell through, opportunities disappeared, things I had worked tirelessly for unravelled before my eyes. At the time, they felt like losses. But looking back, I see them for what they were: redirections.

Not every failure is a failure. Sometimes, it is a necessary step toward something bigger. The challenge is having the patience to see it through.

Legacy is not built in certainty. It is built in persistence. In trusting that every step—even the ones that feel like detours—are shaping something greater than we can yet understand.

People think of legacy as something distant, something that will be evaluated long after they are gone. But that is a dangerous illusion. Legacy is not waiting for you at the end of your life. You are building it now.

Every interaction you have, every conversation, every decision—it all leaves an imprint. The question is, are you shaping that imprint with intention?

I used to think that legacy required extraordinary acts. That it was reserved for people who built empires, wrote history, changed the course of nations. But I was wrong.

The most powerful legacies are not found in history books. They are found in the quiet, ordinary moments. In the way you make people feel. In the lessons you pass down. In the values you uphold, even when no one is watching.

And so, the real question is not: *What will I leave behind?*

The real question is: *Am I proud of the legacy I am shaping right now?*

Because in the end, it will not matter how much wealth you accumulate, how many titles you hold, or how much applause you receive.

The Three Pillars of a Meaningful Legacy

Legacy is often misunderstood. It is imagined as a grand, towering monument, something solid, undeniable, something the world cannot ignore. It is easy to believe that legacy belongs to those who have carved their names into history—leaders who have ruled nations, inventors who have reshaped industries, thinkers who have changed the way we understand the world. But that isn't the full truth. Legacy, real legacy, is quieter. It is built in the unnoticed moments, in the conversations that are long forgotten by the speaker but never forgotten by the listener. It is built in the way you make someone feel when they are uncertain, in the advice you give that sets them on a path they might never have taken otherwise, in the small choices that ripple outward in ways you will never see.

There are three pillars upon which every meaningful legacy is built: impact, influence, and integrity. They are not separate but interwoven, reinforcing one another in a continuous cycle. To understand what you will leave behind, you must first understand what you are building.

Pillar One: Impact – What You Create
Impact is often mistaken for visibility. We are told that impact is measured in numbers, in milestones, in public recognition. That a person's contribution to the world is

determined by how many books they sell, how many followers they accumulate, how widely their work is known. But real impact doesn't announce itself. It doesn't always happen in front of an audience. The greatest impacts are often invisible in the moment they happen.

A teacher who shifts a student's perspective with a single sentence. A mentor who changes the course of someone's life simply by believing in them. A conversation that stops someone from giving up on themselves. Most people who create lasting impact don't realise it in the moment. They are simply moving through the world, doing what they believe is right. They do not see the full weight of their influence because it unfolds over time, across different lives, in ways they will never fully witness. But that does not make it any less real.

There was a moment in my life when I had the chance to make a difference and I hesitated. It wasn't a dramatic moment. There was no life hanging in the balance, no great decision on the line. It was something small—so small that if I hadn't thought about it later, it might have disappeared from my memory entirely.

I was in a conversation with someone who was struggling, someone who was on the edge of a decision that would shape their future. They were searching for direction, and I could see it. I knew I had something to offer, a perspective that might have helped. But I hesitated. I told myself it wasn't my place, that they hadn't asked for advice, that perhaps they wouldn't listen anyway.

And so, I said nothing.

I don't know what happened after that. I don't know if they found their way or if they continued to struggle. But that moment stayed with me—not as regret, but as a lesson. Impact doesn't wait for perfect timing. It doesn't ask whether you feel ready or whether you are certain your words will be received. It happens in the small moments, the unnoticed decisions, the times when you choose to step up even when no one will remember that you did.

That lesson changed the way I move through the world. It taught me that legacy isn't something you build later, when you feel prepared, when you have enough experience or influence or confidence. It is something you build now. What you choose to do today will outlive you. The ideas you share, the kindness you extend, the values you reinforce—these things will continue to exist long after you are gone. That is the nature of impact. It is not defined by its scale, but by its depth.

And so, the question is not whether you will leave a legacy. You will. The question is whether you will shape it intentionally or allow it to form by accident.

What is the problem in the world that keeps you awake at night? Who do you feel most called to help? What is the message, the gift, the lesson you want to pass on? These are not theoretical questions. They are the foundation of what you are building every day, whether you realise it or not. If you had to define your impact—the lasting imprint you want to leave behind—what would it be?

The impact is never insignificant. It is never wasted. It is never forgotten, even if you never see the full extent of what you have built.

Pillar Two: Influence – Who You Inspire

There is a moment that sneaks up on you when you least expect it. A message from someone you barely remember. A chance encounter with a former student, a past colleague, an old acquaintance. And they tell you something that stops you in your tracks.

"You probably don't remember this, but something you said years ago completely changed the way I thought about my work."

"I never told you this, but that one conversation we had pushed me to finally start my business."

"You didn't realise it at the time, but the way you handled that situation taught me everything I needed to know about leadership."

And suddenly, you realise something astonishing. Influence is not about control. It is not about persuading, convincing, or commanding. It is about planting seeds that grow in ways you may never witness. The most powerful influence does not come from force but from example. It does not happen in moments of performance but in moments of presence.

The greatest leaders, the ones who truly shift the world, don't just succeed themselves. They elevate others. They move through life creating space for people to step into their own power, to find their own path, to become more than they ever thought possible. The irony is that true influence is rarely visible. It often happens in whispers rather than in declarations. It unfolds in the quiet spaces between action and reaction, between what we intend and what is actually received. And because we don't always see its effects, we often underestimate it.

When I step onto a stage to deliver a keynote, I am acutely aware of this. My audience is not looking for abstract theories or strategies they could find in a hundred different books. They are looking for something real—lived experience, tangible insights, something they can carry with them when they leave the room. That is the difference between knowledge and influence. One fills the mind; the other moves the soul.

The moments that matter most are not the ones spent delivering a perfect speech. They are the moments that come after. The quiet conversations with audience members who linger when the applause has died down, their eyes lit with realisation. The ones who say, "I never thought about it like that before." The ones who decide, in that instant, to take action.

That is where influence begins—not in the talk itself, but in the spark it ignites.

"Influence is not about control—it is about planting seeds that grow in ways you may never witness." – Unknown

And the thing about influence is that it doesn't stop with the first interaction. It moves outward, multiplying itself in ways no one can predict. Someone hears something, takes action, and passes that knowledge on to someone else. A shift in perspective in one person turns into a shift in behaviour in another. Influence creates ripples that extend far beyond our line of sight.

But we forget this. We assume that if we cannot see our influence, it must not exist. We measure impact only in what is immediately visible. And in doing so, we diminish the weight of our own presence in the world.

So, take a moment to trace the ripples of your own influence. Who has shaped the way you think, the way you work, the way you lead? If you follow that thread back far enough, you'll see that your greatest inspirations may not have been people with grand titles or public recognition. They may have been the ones who, in an ordinary moment, made you feel seen. They may have been the ones who asked the right question at the right time. Who believed in you when you didn't yet believe in yourself.

And now, consider this: You are playing that role in someone else's life. Right now.

The challenge is to do it with intention. To recognise that the smallest actions—offering encouragement, giving someone the benefit of the doubt, leading by example rather than by command—are the very things that create the most lasting impact.

Pillar Three: Integrity – How You Live

There are two kinds of legacies. The ones that shine briefly, built on ambition and skill but lacking the weight to endure. And the ones that last, not because of what was achieved but because of how it was done. Integrity is the difference. A legacy built on deception or self-interest crumbles the moment someone sees behind the curtain. No matter how grand the accomplishments, no matter how far influence spreads, if the foundation is weak, it will not hold.

In a world that constantly rewards results, integrity is often overlooked. People celebrate the finish line, the achievement, the breakthrough, rarely questioning what it took to get there. But history remembers differently. We remember the ones who stood for something, the ones who didn't trade their values for a shortcut, the ones whose principles outlived them.

There is something powerful about a person who moves through life with unwavering integrity. Not the loud, performative kind that demands attention, but the quiet kind that simply is. The leader who refuses to make an easy compromise, even when no one is watching. The entrepreneur who chooses ethics over profit, knowing it may cost them in the short term. The friend who tells the truth when a lie would have been more convenient. These are the people we trust. These are the ones whose legacies endure.

Integrity is not a title you claim. It is something revealed in the smallest of actions. It is in how you speak to someone who can do nothing for you. It is in whether you follow through on a promise no one would have remembered. It is in whether you remain the same person when the cameras are on and when they are off.

There was once a man who could have had everything. He was offered power, wealth, influence beyond measure. But he chose something different. He chose to uphold his principles, even when it cost him. He chose to tell the truth, even when it was unpopular. He chose to walk away from deals that would have made him rich because they did not align with his values. And because of that, the world trusted him. His name carried weight. His legacy, decades later, still shapes lives.

"The strongest legacies are not built on what we do, but on how we do it." – Unknown

It is easy to look at these stories and think of them as extraordinary. To believe that integrity is something reserved for the greats, for historical figures, for people who somehow operate on a different level than the rest of us. But that is the illusion. Integrity does not start with grand gestures. It starts in the daily decisions. It is shaped in the smallest moments, the ones that seem insignificant at the time.

So, the real question is not what you want to achieve. It is how you want to achieve it. If someone were to judge you only by your smallest, daily behaviours, what would they say? If your legacy was not written in your words, but in your choices, what would it reveal?

The Daily Practice of Building a Legacy

The Five-Minute Legacy Builder

Every day presents an opportunity to reinforce the kind of legacy you want to build. The mistake many people make is assuming that legacy is tied to monumental efforts, but in reality, it is the accumulation of small, consistent actions. *The Five-Minute Legacy Builder* is a simple yet powerful way to ensure that your daily choices align with your long-term vision. Each day, take just five minutes to reflect on these three questions:

1. **What is one small action I can take today to reinforce my legacy?**

   Your legacy is built in real time, and each day provides a chance to shape it. This action doesn't have to be grand. It could be as simple as mentoring someone, sharing a lesson, or choosing to respond with patience instead of frustration. Small actions, done consistently, compound over time.

2. **Who can I positively impact before the day is over?**

   Influence and impact are not abstract concepts; they are the direct result of how we engage with others. Whether it is a colleague, a friend, a family member, or even a stranger, every interaction is an opportunity to leave an imprint. Identify at least one person you can encourage, help, or uplift in a meaningful way.

3. **Am I making choices that align with my core values?**

Legacy is not just about what you do, but how you do it. If you claim integrity as a core value, are your daily actions reflecting that? If you want to be remembered for generosity, are you actively practicing it? Take a moment to assess whether your behaviours match the principles you want to be known for.

Designing Your Personal Legacy Plan

Without a clear sense of direction, it is easy to drift and let external forces shape your life instead of actively shaping it yourself. Designing your personal legacy plan helps you identify what you want to be remembered for and how to align your actions with that vision.

Step 1: Define Your Core Values

Your values dictate your legacy. The first step in this process is to write down the three to five values that matter most to you. Consider what truly resonates with you—things like integrity, resilience, compassion, excellence, or service. These will serve as the foundation for everything else.

Step 2: Identify the Areas of Your Life Where You Want to Leave an Impact

Legacy is multidimensional. It extends into your career, relationships, and contributions to the world. Take time to write down the key areas where you want to make a lasting impact. It could be through your professional work, mentorship, philanthropy, or the way you raise your children. The goal is to be intentional about where your influence will be felt the most.

Step 3: Set Intentional Habits That Reinforce Your Desired Legacy

The difference between people who leave a lasting impact and those who don't is their ability to translate intentions into habits. If you want to be known for generosity, set a habit of giving regularly, whether it's your time, knowledge, or resources. If mentorship is part of your legacy, commit to helping someone consistently. Small, repeatable actions create the ripple effect that defines a legacy.

The Legacy Blueprint Worksheet

Once you have reflected on the key elements of your legacy, it is time to put it into a structured plan. *The Legacy Blueprint Worksheet* helps you create a tangible roadmap for living with impact, influence, and integrity.

1. **What principles will guide my daily decisions?**
   These are your non-negotiables. Every action you take should reflect the values you have chosen.

2. **Who do I want to influence, and how?**
   Legacy is not just about what you achieve—it is about who you inspire and elevate along the way. List the people or groups you want to impact and describe how you will do so.

3. **What long-term actions will solidify my legacy?**
   These are the major commitments that will define your impact over time. It could be writing a book, launching a foundation, mentoring a new generation of leaders, or creating something that will outlive you.

4. **What daily habits will ensure I stay aligned with my vision?**

   Habits are the bridge between intentions and reality. Identify small, repeatable actions that will reinforce your legacy daily.

Living Your Legacy Now

Most legacies are not written in history books. They are not carved into marble or preserved in the pages of biographies. They do not come with medals or grand recognitions.

Instead, they live quietly in the memories of the people whose lives were changed by something seemingly small. The teacher who sparked a lifelong passion in a student. The friend who offered support in a moment of doubt. The stranger who gave kindness when someone needed it most.

The world does not track these moments. It does not record them or celebrate them. But that does not make them any less real.

Think back to your own life. The moments that changed you, the words that stayed with you, the acts of kindness that you never forgot. The people who may not even realise that they left a mark on you. Now consider this: Right now, in this moment, you are leaving marks on others in the same way. You may not see it. You may never know it. But your actions, your words, your presence—they matter more than you can imagine.

That is the weight of legacy. It is not something we leave behind after we are gone. It is something we are shaping, moment by moment, in the way we choose to live.

Everything I have shared with you in this book is simple. Not easy—but simple. No one step is insurmountable. The real question is not whether you can do it. The question is, do you want it? And if so, are you willing to go after it?

If you take nothing else from this book, take this:

You don't need more time, more money, or more influence. You just need to choose.

So, the only question left is this:

Are you building it with intention?

"We are remembered not for what we have, but for what we give. Not for the battles we win, but for the lives we change. True immortality is found not in monuments or titles, but in the hearts of those we leave better than we found them." – Unknown

CHAPTER 10

WHEN GIVING FELT LIKE LOSING

——•◦◇◦•——

She carried herself as if kindness were an unbreakable law of nature, as if giving was something written into her very being, something she had no choice but to do. It was not for recognition or validation. It was not a performance of goodness. It was woven into her identity, something deeper than obligation, more instinctive than calculation. She went out of her way to care for others, not because she expected anything in return, but because it was simply who she was. She reached out instinctively, without hesitation. She held space for others, whether or not they asked for it. Her kindness was not transactional—it was a quiet, steady presence that asked for nothing and gave everything. She travelled across the world to visit and care for others knowing never to expect anything in return. Yet none of it held her back.

There was an elegance in it, a quiet power. Her generosity was not conditional, nor was it diminished by circumstance. It came from a place of abundance, a belief that kindness was something to be given freely, without measure.

As a child and for much of my adult life, I struggled to make sense of it. It defied logic—the idea that giving was worthwhile even when there were no guarantees. That kindness was something you offered, not because of how it would be received, but because of who you were. I searched for an equation that would make it make sense. That giving should lead to receiving, that care should be mirrored in return. But my mother did not follow those rules. She gave, and she kept giving, because it was simply in her nature.

I saw it in the small moments—the way she prepared meals with care, the way she made space for others, the way she remained steady in her goodness no matter what life placed in her path. I did not understand it then. I wanted her to guard herself, to give only where she was sure it would be returned.

But she never did. And she never explained why.

She saw the world differently. To her, generosity was not about guarantees—it was about being true to herself.

In forty days, she lost her mother, her father, and her sis-
ter—three pillars of love and familiarity. Yet even in the
face of such profound loss, she held on to who she was.
I was too young to remember those days, too young to
understand the weight of her loss. But as I grew older,
the echoes of that time became part of our family's story.
Relatives would talk about how she faced each day,
when her world was falling apart.

I imagined her in those moments—her shoulders heavy
with sorrow, her heart fractured in ways that no one
could see. I imagined her alone at night, tears silently es-
caping, her hands clasped as if holding on to fragments
of hope. Yet, she continued to give, continued to love,
continued to believe.

Her wisdom wasn't born from invincibility; it was forged
through grief and resilience. She taught me that true
strength is not about never breaking; it's about finding
the courage to rebuild, piece by piece. She showed me
that generosity is not the absence of pain, but the refusal
to let pain dictate who you become. Her giving was a
choice—a defiance against despair.

She never let sorrow define her, never let absence diminish the way she showed up for others. She remained
open, generous, steadfast. And I did not understand it. I
did not recognise the strength it takes to keep giving, to

keep loving, even when the world has given you every reason not to.

I wanted answers. Why? Why continue to pour into others with no certainty of what would come back? Why invest in places where the outcome was unknown? Why keep giving when the world teaches us to protect, to withhold, to make sure we are not left empty-handed?

She never explained. She never needed to. She just kept living as she always had—giving not for recognition, but because it was her nature. Because for her, kindness was not a question of whether it was deserved, but a reflection of who she chose to be.

As a mother, she gave without hesitation, without rest, without expectation. She carried more than we ever realised—our worries, our uncertainties, the weight of our futures—shielding us from burdens we never even knew existed. She sacrificed quietly, never speaking of what she let go of so that we could have more. Her time, her dreams, even her own comfort—she placed them all second to what we needed.

She loved with a strength that never wavered, with an energy that felt endless. No matter how much she had already given, no matter how exhausted she must have been, she always found more to give. Because for her, we weren't just a responsibility. We were her world.

It took years before I realised that she wasn't losing. She was not operating by the rules of transactions, of measured exchanges. She was playing a different game entirely.

She was not making transactions.

She was making investments.

It was not about what she would get back in the immediate moment, in the obvious ways. It was about something bigger, something I could not yet see.

And the day I understood that, I was no longer thinking about her.

I was thinking about myself.

The first time I gave—really gave—without getting anything back, I felt it. That creeping feeling of exhaustion, of resentment. The feeling of being taken for granted. The bitterness of realising that people often only remember you when they need something. That they take your presence for granted. That they assume you will always be there.

And I did not like it.

I did not like how it made me question whether generosity was worth it. I did not like how it made me second-guess acts that should have been natural. I did not like how giving felt like losing.

And then, in that moment, clear as day, I heard my mother's voice.

"We don't give to get back from people. We give because our return isn't written here."

And I understood. She had never been giving for them. She had been giving for us.

She gives so that we—her children, her family, the next generation—never feel the loneliness she endured. She takes the absence she once felt and turns it into a presence that continues to shape us. She is planting something she never expects to bloom in her lifetime, but she plants it anyway.

I realised then that my mother's giving was never just about people. It was about something greater. She understood what I had only just begun to grasp—that we do not give for the validation of the world, we give because our return is written with Allah. And that is why she never wavered.

And suddenly, what once seemed like loss now looked like power.

The power of choosing who you are, regardless of who the world is to you. The power of deciding that your

kindness is not dependent on other people's reciprocation.

My mother had been right all along.

And I had been measuring loss in the wrong way. Because sometimes, the things that seem like losses are actually the most powerful moves of all. And that is a kind
of strength most people will never understand. It took me
a long time to see that real generosity isn't about what
we get back but about what we build in the process. And
that's a lesson far bigger than just my own story—it is
something that shapes the way we all navigate the world.

The Strength of Generosity in a
Transactional World

There is a moment when generosity stops feeling like
virtue and starts feeling like exhaustion. When you have
given and given and yet the world seems indifferent to
your efforts. When you pick up the phone before they
call, when you extend kindness that never circles back.
It is the moment when you sit in the quiet and ask yourself, *What was the point of it all?*

I have been in that moment many times. And every time,
resentment tried to slip in, like an uninvited guest, whispering in my ear that maybe I had been foolish. That

maybe I had been too soft. That maybe the world belonged to those who took rather than those who gave. It was easy to believe, too. The world rewards the shrewd, the ones who negotiate their worth, who never give without ensuring they will receive. We are told that self-preservation is the mark of intelligence. That giving without return is naive. That kindness, in excess, is a flaw.

But then, in the middle of that storm, I would hear her voice. My mother's voice. The quiet, steady certainty of it.

"We don't give to get back from people."

She had been right all along.

The world tells us that strength is in withholding. That wisdom is in knowing when to walk away. That power belongs to those who do not give too freely. But I have come to understand that this is only half the truth. Strength is not just about self-preservation. Real strength is in giving—and giving again—even when the world does not return the favour.

Some of the most influential figures in history gave without ever seeing the full impact of their actions. They planted seeds knowing they would never sit in the shade. They invested in people, in ideas, in movements, not because they expected immediate return, but because they understood that the world is built on the silent work of those who give anyway.

So, what if we measured giving differently? What if we did not measure it by what we lost, but by what it made us? What if we saw every act of generosity, not as something we handed over to another, but as something we built within ourselves?

The Reality of One-Sided Giving—And How to Handle It Without Losing Yourself

Why should I keep giving when no one gives back? Why should I care when it feels like no one else does?

But what if these are the wrong questions?

What if the real power isn't in what we get back from others—but in what we become when we give?

When you give without keeping score, you free yourself from the exhaustion of expectation. You become someone who is not controlled by whether others reciprocate. You move beyond the fragile, transaction-based view of generosity that so many people live by. You begin to understand that real kindness is not about what you receive—it is about what you build.

And yet, this does not mean that giving should be limit-less. Even the most selfless people have boundaries. Even those who give the most must learn when to step back. My mother, for all her endless generosity, had her quiet limits. There were moments when she withdrew. Not loudly. Not angrily. Just enough to remind herself that her kindness was a choice, not an obligation.

There is a balance to be found—a way to give without feeling drained, a way to offer kindness without becoming bitter. It begins with a shift in perspective. Instead of asking, "Why does no one give back?" ask yourself:

Who am I becoming through this?

Is this an investment in something bigger?

Am I giving in places where my generosity is planting something real?

Because not every imbalance is unfair. Some are invest-ments. The key is knowing which ones are worth mak-ing.

There are ways to give without losing yourself. The first is to stop treating generosity like a debt ledger. The fast-est way to feel exhausted is to keep track of everything you have given, measuring it against what has been re-turned. There is no joy in that kind of giving. There is only resentment. Instead of asking, "What have I gotten back?" ask, "What have I built through my giving?"

Giving should never mean tolerating mistreatment. You can be generous without being a doormat. You can be kind without allowing people to take advantage of you. The difference is in knowing where to redirect your energy. Not every place you pour into will grow something worthwhile. Not every person you invest in will appreciate the effort. But some will. And those are the places, the people, the moments worth focusing on.

One of the hardest truths to accept is that not all kindness will be recognised. Some of the most meaningful things you do will go unnoticed. Some of the biggest sacrifices you make will be unacknowledged. But just because something is unseen does not mean it is lost. The right moments, the right people, the right opportunities—they find their way back to you. Maybe not in the way you expected. Maybe not from the places you first gave. But nothing is wasted. Not a single act of goodness disappears.

And sometimes, the person we neglect most in our giving is ourselves. It is easy to become so focused on what we are offering to others that we forget to offer the same generosity to ourselves. Selflessness is powerful—but it should never come at the expense of self-respect. You, too, deserve the patience, the kindness, the forgiveness that you so freely give to others.

Finally, there comes a time when you must let go of the people who do not see your worth. There are those who will never appreciate what you bring, no matter how much you offer. And that is okay. True self-respect is knowing when to stop expecting from those who have nothing to give.

Generosity is not weakness. It is not naivety. It is not foolishness. It is a choice. A strength. A reflection of who you are, not of what others do in return. And in the end, that is what truly matters.

Because some losses are actually the most powerful wins.

Her life is a testament to the power of giving, even when it feels like losing. And as I continue to walk my own path, I see the truth she lives by: that real strength is in choosing who you are, regardless of what life takes away. Her quiet courage shapes me every day, not just as her daughter but as a leader. Even now, she continues to teach me that strength is not about never falling—it's about the choice to rise again, to give again, to lead again. Her legacy is not just in the past; it's alive in every act of kindness, in every decision to be better, to be

braver. And as you navigate your own challenges, remember her example. Because sometimes the most powerful wins come from the moments that felt like losing.
Especially then.

The Legacy of Unseen Giving

She never lost. That was the realisation that settled over
me, years too late. I had spent my childhood watching,
unable to comprehend why she kept giving to people
who never gave back. I had grown into adulthood resent-
ing the imbalance, tallying up the moments of her unnoticed sacrifices, the times she had gone out of her way to
be there for someone who wouldn't do the same for her.
I saw generosity as a game of fairness, a simple equation
of effort in, reward out. And in that equation, she should
have lost. But she never did.

She never lost because she was never playing by the rules
I thought mattered. She was never measuring her worth
by the appreciation of others, never keeping a ledger of
who owed her what, never allowing the lack of reciprocation to change who she was. Her giving was not a strategy. It was not a tool to gain favour or ensure loyalty. It
was simply the way she existed in the world. And that, I
realise now, is the greatest kind of strength.

The world tells us that power lies in taking, in accumulating, in ensuring we are not left empty-handed. We are told to be smart about where we invest our time, our energy, our care. We are warned not to waste kindness on those who won't return it. We learn to protect ourselves from disappointment, from the pain of giving to those who do not appreciate it. We build walls around our hearts, thinking we are keeping ourselves safe, when really, we are only shrinking the space where love could have grown.

But my mother never built those walls. She never let the world make her smaller. She never let other people's indifference dictate her actions. And because of that, she was free in a way most of us will never be.

That is the legacy of unseen giving. The kindness that goes unnoticed but is never wasted. The sacrifices that are not acknowledged but are still felt. The love that is given freely, not because it is deserved, but because withholding it would make you someone you don't want to be.

We are not remembered for what we have. We are remembered for what we give.

And yet, we live in a world that measures everything by what can be seen, what can be counted. Money, accomplishments, accolades—these are the things that define success in the eyes of society. But the real impact of a life is not found in numbers. It is found in the spaces between them. The quiet gestures that shifted someone's path. The moments of kindness that were never spoken of but were never forgotten either. The unseen ways in which one life touches another, and then another, and then another, until the ripple effect has stretched farther than anyone could have predicted.

Not a single act of kindness is wasted.

There is a verse in the Qur'an that echoes this truth: "And whatever you spend of good – it will be fully repaid to you, and you will not be wronged" (2:272).

That is the only guarantee worth holding onto. Not that people will always appreciate your giving. Not that the world will always be fair. But that every act of goodness is accounted for, every sacrifice is seen, and nothing you pour into the world is ever truly lost.

The challenge, then, is not to decide whether giving is worth it. It is. The challenge is to decide *who you will be* in a world that does not always value generosity. Will you allow the disappointment of others to harden you? Will you let the lack of reciprocation change you? Will you build walls around your heart, making sure you never give more than you receive?

Or will you choose to give anyway?

To love, even when it isn't returned in equal measure.

To show up, even when no one is keeping track.

To be kind, not because the world will always repay you, but because you refuse to become someone who withholds goodness.

And so now, when I give, I do it differently than I used to. I no longer expect the return to come in ways I can predict. I no longer keep a running tally in my head. I give, not because I am waiting for people to give back, but because I trust that my return is already written.

Some people give to receive. Others give because they know that giving, in itself, is enough.

The world may forget what you gave. But He never will.

So if you have ever felt like your generosity was wasted, if you have ever wondered whether all the effort, the love, the kindness you have poured into others was worth it—trust me.

Not a single drop was lost.

And that is what my mother has taught me—not through words but through the way she has lived. That giving is not about what we lose but about who we become. That kindness is not measured by the reactions of others but by the impact it leaves behind, whether seen or unseen.

I have spent years learning, unlearning, and relearning what it truly means to give. Not just in kindness but in knowledge, in wisdom, in the experiences I have gathered along the way. And I have given it all away—not because I had to but because I could. Because the only way for these lessons to live on is to pass them forward, to plant them in the lives of others so they can take root and grow in places I may never see.

This journey has shaped me in ways I never could have imagined. It has taken me through doubt, through resistance, through the quiet ache of wondering whether it was all worth it. And then, through realisation—one too precious to keep to myself. That to give is not to diminish but to expand. That what we offer to others does not leave us with less, it leaves us with more. More understanding, more strength, more purpose.

And perhaps that is the greatest lesson of all. That in the end, we are not remembered for what we kept. We are remembered for what we gave away.

So, as I reflect on everything I have learned—the lessons that have shaped me, the struggles that have moulded me, the moments that have brought me closer to Allah— I know one truth above all else.

A Personal Tribute

First and foremost, I thank Allah, the Almighty, the One who never turns away, the One who listens when no one else does. The One who responds even in the quietest moments of our despair. I thank Him for guiding me when I could not see the way, for making the path easy when I thought it was impossible, for answering me in ways I did not even realise I needed.

Because I did not just find answers in my mother's giving. I found them in my darkest moments—the moments when I felt unseen, unheard, questioning whether all the effort, all the love, all the sacrifice was worth it. The moments when I stood at a crossroads, unsure where the path ahead was leading me, when no one around me had the answers, when no guidance seemed clear. But even then, Allah was there. When no one else could navigate the way for me, He made way for a path.

Because you cannot say you tried everything if you have never woken up in the last third of the night to ask Allah for it. You cannot say you searched for every answer if you have never turned to Him when the world was asleep, when the distractions were gone, when it was just you and the One who always listens. I learned that true effort is not just in what we do with our hands, but in what we surrender in *sujood*. I learned that even in the depths of uncertainty, when every door seemed closed, the doors to Allah were always open. And when I knocked on them, I found ease where I thought there would only be struggle. I found clarity where there had been confusion. I found guidance when I thought I was lost.

And I know now that Allah's greatest blessing to me, after faith itself, is the parents He gave me. He placed me in the hands of two extraordinary people who shaped not only my childhood, but the very core of who I am.

It is through His wisdom that He chose them for me, knowing exactly the lessons I needed, the love that would shape me, the guidance that would prepare me for the journey ahead. Every sacrifice they made, every act of love, every moment of strength—they were reflections of Allah's mercy, His favour, His divine plan. They gave selflessly because they believed in His provision. They loved unconditionally because they trusted in His protection. And for that, my gratitude to Him is endless.

Mum, there is not a day that passes when I do not thank Allah that I am your daughter. To be raised by you, to be loved by you, to have the privilege of calling you my mum is the greatest blessing of my life.

You and Dad have been our foundation—each of you shaping us in different, yet equally profound ways. His strength, his wisdom, his unwavering support have guided us, but it is your heart, your boundless kindness, your quiet yet unstoppable resilience that has taught us the meaning of unconditional love. You have carried so much, given so selflessly, and held us together in ways we never fully realised. You have been our comfort, our teacher, our safe place.

Your strength is unmatched, your wisdom a light that has guided us through every storm. You give without hesitation, love without limits, and pour yourself into the world in ways that continue to inspire us every single day. You never cease to amaze us. Your brilliance, your grace, your unwavering heart—every moment, you remind us of what true greatness looks like.

It is the greatest honour of my life to be your daughter and nothing will ever come close. To have been raised by you and Dad, to have been shaped by your love, your values, and your unwavering strength, is a privilege beyond words. Together, you built a home filled with warmth, faith, and purpose—a home where love was never questioned, where sacrifice was given without hesitation, and where we were always safe. Though Dad is no longer with us, his presence lives on in everything you both created, in the lessons you instilled and in the love that continues to surround us because of you.

It was Allah's mercy that made you both my parents. It was His guidance that nurtured your wisdom, His love that filled your hearts, His light that illuminated your paths. Through you, He showed me what faith in action looks like. And so, my gratitude to Him deepens with every memory, every lesson, every act of love.

And Mum, through it all, you remain the heart of every-thing. The one who carries forward not just his memory, but the legacy of both of you, with the same grace, wis-dom, and quiet strength that has always defined you. You have given us more than we will ever be able to put into words. And I can only hope to honour that by carrying forward even a fraction of what you and Dad have built. If I can live with the same love, the same grace, the same quiet strength that you have shown us every single day, then I will know I have done something right. Because everything I am, and everything I hope to be, is shaped by you.

Through every storm and every triumph, I have come to understand that my journey is but a reflection of Allah's mercy and guidance. And I pray that I carry forward the legacy He entrusted to me, with the same faith, the same courage, and the same unwavering belief in Him that you both exemplified. For in every moment, every success, and every lesson, I am reminded that it is Allah who guides, Allah who protects, and Allah who never leaves us, even when the world does.

Alhamdulillah.

Epilogue

THE DECISION THAT CHANGES EVERYTHING

––––––•◦◇◦•––––––

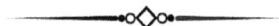

S ome books are meant to be read. Others are meant to be *lived.*

If you have made it this far, you already know that this was never just a collection of ideas. It was never meant to be a comfortable read, something to pass the time before returning to life as you knew it. This was a challenge—one that asked you to question everything you have been told about success, leadership, and power.

Because the truth is, the world does not belong to those who wait. It does not belong to those who hesitate, hoping that someone will recognise their potential and hand them an opportunity. It does not belong to those who seek permission before acting. The world belongs to those who understand that waiting is the most dangerous decision of all. That doors do not open unless you push

292

them. That clarity does not come before action—it follows it.

You were never bound by the expectations placed on you. You were never obligated to follow the rules that were designed to keep you in place. But here is the thing about systems—they only work if you comply. The moment you refuse to accept them as unchangeable, you start to see them for what they are: constructs, not constraints.

And now, after everything you have read, the question remains: *Will you step forward? Or will you hold yourself back?*

This journey began on an afternoon like any other. Except it wasn't. Because everything changed.

The kind of change that does not ask for permission. The kind that arrives unannounced, stripping away the illusions of certainty and leaving you with one question: will you rise, or will you retreat? That moment was not about leadership alone. It was about stepping into discomfort before you were ready—because that is where transformation begins.

From there, you dismantled the outdated playbook. You saw for yourself that waiting for permission, waiting for the right time, waiting for someone to pave the way—that is the greatest risk of all. Because while you wait, others move. And the moment you decide to take action, no matter how imperfect, you are already ahead of those still searching for signs.

You learned that growth is not about safety. It is not about staying within familiar lines. It is about stepping into spaces where you feel unqualified, speaking when your voice shakes, standing your ground even when you are questioned. Growth is about challenging the system—not for the sake of rebellion, but for the sake of something greater.

And then, the breaking points arrived. The exhaustion, the doubt, the feeling of being stretched too thin. The moments where everything felt impossible. But now you know—breaking points are not endings. They are beginnings. The moment you feel lost is often the moment just before the breakthrough. You do not need to fear struggle. Struggle is the cost of growth.

Success is not a sprint. Nor is it just about working hard. Because effort alone does not guarantee outcomes. Success is about strategy. It is about knowing when to push, when to pause, when to pivot. It is about creating a system that does not just work *for you*—but works *without you,* so that success is not something you chase, but something you sustain.

And failure? It was never the enemy. Failure is only fatal to those who refuse to learn from it. You have now seen that the real danger is not in making mistakes. The real danger is in *hesitation,* in the slow erosion of belief in yourself, in waiting so long that opportunities pass before you even reach for them. The only people who never fail are the ones who never try.

You understand now that leadership is not about dominance. It is about momentum. It is about trust. It is about knowing that real influence is not built through control or authority—it is built through clarity, through presence, through the ability to *shape* the conversations that matter.

And beyond leadership, beyond success, beyond strategy—you now understand that legacy is not something that happens at the end. Legacy is built *now,* in the way you choose to show up, in the choices you make daily, in the way you impact others, even when no one is watching.

Perhaps the most important lesson of all.

In a world obsessed with transactions, obsessed with what is gained and what is lost, obsessed with measuring worth in numbers, true power lies in generosity.

Not every return is immediate. Not every investment is seen. Not every effort is recognised. But nothing you give—your knowledge, your time, your presence—is ever wasted.

You may never see the impact of what you create. But that does not mean the impact does not exist.

The most powerful people in history were not the ones who took the most. They were the ones who *gave the most*. Not because they expected something in return, but because they understood a fundamental truth:

Power is not about what you hold. It is about what you pass on.

And that is the legacy I hope you take forward.

This book is not just my story; it is more than that. It reflects the path we all walk—the moments of doubt, the battles with fear, the journey of stepping into something greater than ourselves. It was never meant to be read and then forgotten. It was meant to challenge you, to move you, to shift something deep inside you.

If something in these pages resonated, if something changed the way you see yourself or the path ahead, then let me say this: I would love to hear from you. Tell me what changed. Tell me what decision you are no longer postponing. Tell me what action you are taking now that you are no longer waiting for permission.

I have been blessed. Not because life has been easy, but because I have had the chance to learn, to experience, to grow. And as I wrote these pages, one question stayed with me—the same question we will all be asked one day:

What did you do with what you were given?

And when my time here is done and I stand before my Creator, I want to be able to say:

"My Lord, I passed it on. Every lesson, every hardship, every ounce of knowledge, experience, and wisdom You blessed me with—I did not keep it for myself. I gave it freely so that others could rise. Not so they could be like me, but so they could be better than me."

Because that is the purpose of every lesson we learn— not to keep it, but to pass it forward.

To leave the world *richer. Wiser. Better than we found it.*

That is the real measure of success.

Not the accolades. Not the titles. Not the fleeting moments of recognition.

But the lives we impact.

You now know what it takes to break through. The courage to step forward before you are ready. The resilience to keep going even when the path is unclear. The clarity to define success on your terms.

If you have reached this point, you are already ahead of those still waiting for the right moment.

The real question is:

What will you do next?

Your next bold move does not have to be perfect.

It just has to be taken.

This book was written from the heart. I hope you felt that in every page.

And there is more to come. More lessons. More stories. More breakthroughs.

But before I write that next chapter, I need to know—is this the book you needed? Has it given you what you were searching for?

Your journey, your transformation, your story will shape what comes next.

Until then—**step forward.**

Do not wait for permission.

Do not wait for certainty.

Do not wait for someone to tell you it is your time.

It already is.

Rewrite your own win.

With gratitude,

Bibliography

Arkes, H. R., & Blumer, C. (1985). The psychology of sunk cost. *Organizational Behavior and Human Decision Processes, 35*(1), 124–140.

Asch, S. E. (1951). Effects of group pressure upon the modification and distortion of judgments. In H. Guetzkow (Ed.), *Groups, leadership and men* (pp. 177–190). Carnegie Press.

Bandura, A. (1977). Self-efficacy: Toward a unifying theory of behavioral change. *Psychological Review, 84*(2), 191–215.

Feynman, R. P. (1985). *Surely You're Joking, Mr. Feynman!* (Adventures of a Curious Character). W.W. Norton & Company.

Holiday, R. (2014). *The obstacle is the way: The timeless art of turning trials into triumph.* Portfolio.

Huffington, A. (2014). *Thrive: The third metric to redefining success and creating a life of well-being, wisdom, and wonder.* Harmony Books.

Isaacson, W. (2011). *Steve Jobs.* Simon & Schuster.

Kahneman, D., & Tversky, A. (1979). Prospect theory: An analysis of decision under risk. *Econometrica, 47*(2), 263–291.

Mandela, N. (1994). *Long walk to freedom: The autobiography of Nelson Mandela.* Little, Brown and Company.

McCullough, D. (2015). *The Wright brothers.* Simon & Schuster.

Ohno, T. (1988). *Toyota Production System: Beyond large-scale production.* Productivity Press.

Tedeschi, R. G., & Calhoun, L. G. (1996). The Posttraumatic Growth Inventory: Measuring the positive legacy of trauma. *Journal of Traumatic Stress, 9*(3), 455–471.

Zeigarnik, B. (1927). Über das Behalten von erledigten und unerledigten Handlungen [On the retention of completed and uncompleted tasks]. *Psychologische Forschung, 9*(1), 1–85.

Reader's Notes

ABOUT THE AUTHOR

Amna Zaidi, FCA CMgr MCMI, is a distinguished British executive, transformational leader, and international speaker with over two decades of experience in banking, financial services, and organisational change. A graduate with honours in Business and Accounting in 2001, she qualified as a Chartered Accountant in 2003, setting the stage for a career defined by resilience, innovation, and a commitment to excellence. At the remarkably young age of 24, Amna shattered glass ceilings by reporting to a company board as the one of the only female, Asian, and Muslim member—a milestone that not only marked her entry into the highest echelons of business but also ignited her passion for championing diversity and inclusion.

Amna's early roles at renowned firms such as Deloitte & Touche, BDO, and Allied Irish Bank provided her with a robust foundation in financial insight and regulatory compliance, while her subsequent leadership positions at prestigious institutions including NatWest Group (formerly RBS), Deutsche Bank, and Lloyds Banking Group honed her expertise in driving transformational change. During her tenure, she adeptly managed budgets exceeding £80 million and led large teams through critical periods of operational redesign and strategic renewal.

She is a Freeman of the City of London, a distinction that reflects her significant contributions to the profession and public life. Amna also contributes to the broader professional community as a committee member of the Audit Registration Committee at the Institute of Chartered Accountants in England & Wales (ICAEW).

Today, Amna specialises in empowering organisations to navigate the complexities of modern business environments through bespoke transformation consulting, dynamic leadership training, and inspirational keynote presentations. She is celebrated for her revolutionary Five Stages of Leadership Design, a framework that transforms setbacks into opportunities for growth and propels leaders to exceed expectations.

Beyond her corporate achievements, Amna is a trained Listening Volunteer with the Samaritans, reflecting her deep commitment to mental health and emotional wellbeing. Through her consultancy and speaking engagements, she continues to inspire a new generation of leaders to embrace innovation, fairness, and sustainability—

ensuring that they not only succeed, but also drive meaningful, lasting change.

Printed in Great Britain
by Amazon

62627867R30184